LIVING AFFINITY

LIVING AFFINITY

❧

Hsing Yun

LANTERN BOOKS • NEW YORK
A DIVISION OF BOOKLIGHT INC.

2004
Lantern Books
One Union Square West, Suite 201
New York, NY 10003

Library of Congress Cataloging-in-Publication Data

Printed in Canada

Xingyun, da shi.
Living affinity / Hsing Yun.
p. cm.
ISBN 1-59056-058-2 (alk. paper)
1. Religious life—Buddhism. I. Title.
BQ5395.X56 2004
294.3'444—dc22
2003020821

printed on 100% post-consumer waste paper, chlorine-free

❧ CONTENTS ❧

❧ INTRODUCTION ❧

Living Affinity

FOR MANY OF US, relationships are the primary concern
and focus of our lives. When our relationships are in
balance and running smoothly, we experience a sense of
well-being and happiness. When our relationships are
fraught with disconnection and distance, we feel lonely
and out of sorts. While we would be extremely happy if
someone offered us a solution that immediately created
complete and everlasting harmony in our relationships,
the truth is that we ourselves already contain this potential—our very being is already the absolute fruition of this
unimaginable potential for intimacy. In *Living Affinity*,
Master Hsing Yun invites us to experience relationships
that extend far beyond what we typically consider close
relationships and helps us to develop relationships not
only with other people, but with everything in our experience of reality. He helps us to understand that it is only the
illusive constructs of our mind and our perpetual insistence on viewing ourselves as separate and distinct from

everything around us that inhibit us from having living affinity every moment, with all things. Inherent in every person, Master Hsing Yun argues, is the unblemished and unrestricted ability to awaken affinity in every aspect of our lives.

In Buddhism, the concept of "affinity" transcends our common definition of the term, which is typically understood as a sympathy or liking for someone or something. As it is discussed in this book, "affinity" (the Chinese term is *yuan*) means a profound spiritual relationship that prevails and deepens over many lifetimes. Affinity is not fleeting; it does not come and go. Affinity is the natural state of existence, it is the beginningless and endless hum of the universe; it is the very essence of our being.

Key to understanding our true capacity for affinity is realizing the truth of interdependence. The Buddha taught us that nothing can exist independently—everything is linked through interdependence and nothing can arise outside of relationship. It then follows that by the mere fact of existence, we are in a natural state of affinity with all things. It is both comforting and encouraging that we do not have to struggle or devise a complex plan in order to experience affinity. We only need to reorient our angles of thought and perception that blind us to our true nature in order to reveal the living affinity that always was and always will be. Within this book, we encounter specific practices, wise suggestions, and inspiring examples that can help us in this endeavor.

While the following pages explore affinity in love relationships, friendships, and communities, Master Hsing Yun also encourages and instructs us to cultivate the heart and mind of affinity with the environment, the material world, money, space, time, and, most fundamentally, our spiritual journey. In one comedic, yet entirely sincere, moment we are even inspired to nurture affinity with our dishtowels!

The expanse of Master Hsing Yun's vision and the strength of his leadership have yielded—and continue to yield—extraordinary results. With his tireless energy and remarkable affinity, he has established temples, universities, schools, and other organizations all over the world. His travels have taken him around the globe, where he has developed relationships with countless people from diverse backgrounds and different religious affiliations. His life admirably embodies the saying, "With affinity, people will meet even if they are a thousand miles apart."

Living Affinity is a wonderful gift and a heartfelt guidebook for all who wish to explore the vast range and unlimited potential of relationship. Deep and abiding connections are simmering just below the surface of a flimsy and illusory disguise of our own creation. May you experience peace and joy as you develop a rich spiritual life, and may you delight in becoming the truth of living affinity.

Brenda Bolinger
Staff Writer
The Claremont Courier

CHAPTER ONE

Living Affinity in Community
The Web of Human Relationships

Human beings are social animals; we cannot live apart from community. As Buddhists, we are told to seek the Dharma among the people, for the Dharma does not exist in some other world or faraway place; the Dharma is here among us, embodied in each and every being. Thus, Buddhists understand what many other people from other religious traditions also know: that the cornerstone of happy living is to develop good relationships and nurture positive affinity with others. When we understand that human society is nothing other than a web of human relationships, we will understand just how crucial our relationships are. Each link in the web, or each person in a community, affects the whole. Relationships create a particular atmosphere within a community and determine whether the community—be it a neighborhood, a place of

1

religious gathering, a family, or a different form of community—invites mutual benefit and harmony or leaves its members in a state of isolation and conflict. Once we see how the repercussions of even one relationship can impact an entire community, we will learn to treasure each relationship and invest our most sincere and open efforts in creating relationships that are healthy and beneficial. Wholesome actions are the seeds of good relationships, while unwholesome actions breed problems in our relationships with others. It is important for us to remember that we all have a key role to play in maintaining the health and well-being of this interlocking web.

We also need to understand that human relationships, like all phenomena, develop within the truth that, as the *Treatise on the Perfection of Great Wisdom* says, "All worldly phenomena arise out of causes and conditions; all worldly phenomena cease because of causes and conditions." What this means is that the world is the culmination of our collective karma and conditions for being, and therefore, we all exist on an equal plane; no one has any special circumstances or advantages. Each one of us is born into this world because of our own individual causes and conditions, but the fact that we all live in this world together means that we share some common causes and conditions. How you conduct yourself within relationships will have immeasurable influence on the lives of others, and vice versa, for relationships actually create the conditions of life that we all share. Because of our collective karma and conditions, it is impossible for us to think simply in terms of our own individual happiness and peace. We may try to exist within a community under such personal and self-serving terms, but this inevitably leads to suffering and impedes the nourishment of affinity. In the following pages, I will offer some suggestions about how we can build affinity and live in harmony as we nurture our relationships within the community. To serve this purpose, we will examine many different aspects of the four great all-embracing virtues, the six points of reverent harmony, and the concept of grounding ourselves, and thereby our communities, in oneness.

The four great all-embracing virtues

If we want to understand what the Dharma teaches us about building affinity and living in harmony with others, we must first understand the four great all-embracing virtues. The Buddha teaches that for us to realize our true capacity of connecting with and serving our fellow citizens, we have to first build a good rapport, and the four virtues are tools to that end. The four virtues are: giving, speaking with kind words, conducting oneself for the benefit of others, and adapting oneself to others.

Despite the fact that there are obvious and limitless benefits to practicing the first virtue of giving, many of us choose to lead our lives in a merely self-centered and self-satisfying way. We are often reluctant to put others ahead of ourselves, choosing instead to focus on our own comfort and success. Competition to be the best and have the most permeates contemporary society, making it quite challenging at times to regard the welfare of others as our primary concern. We strive to be better than others, and we often measure the quality of our life by how we compare with those around us. This worldview is the root cause of human conflict and prevents us from being generous to each other. People who are so focused on their own survival and status have no qualms about taking; however, when it is their turn to give, they make all kinds of excuses. If we deeply understand and apply the Buddha's teachings on the truth of life and the universe, we will change our ways; our natural tendency will be to give to others and not take from them. If we understand that every cause has its effect, and that we all share common causes and conditions, then we may think differently about taking advantage of others, and we will not be so hesitant about giving. The following story was taken from Buddhist literature to help us open our eyes to the true meaning of the saying that we are sometimes unwilling to accept: "It is better to give than to receive."

Once, there were two men from the same village; one of them was miserly while the other was generous. They both happened to pass away at about the same time. In death, they appeared before King Yama, who was about to pass judgment on their past actions. He told the two men, "I am going to let both of you be reborn into the world. One of you will always be giving, while the other will always be receiving. Which one would you rather be?"

The miserly person immediately spoke up, "I want to be the one that will always be receiving."

The other man did not mind being the one who would continually be giving, and so he nodded in agreement. Both of them stood waiting for final instructions about where they would be reborn. King Yama picked up his staff and pounded on the ground a few times. He said to the miser, "Since you choose to be receiving from others, you will be reborn as a beggar. This will give you plenty of opportunity to be on the receiving end." He then turned to the other man and said, "You will be reborn into great wealth. Share your wealth with those less fortunate and give alms." The two men learned a poignant lesson from King Yama's clever decision: the experience of giving is much more fulfilling than that of receiving.

Some of you may wonder how you can practice giving if you do not have any money or possessions. How do we build affinity with others through generosity if we have nothing? Actually, we do not need to have great wealth, or even any money at all, to practice the virtue of giving. When you meet someone on the road, give the person a nod or a smile. This is giving. If you help someone who has fallen down, this is also giving. When we show concern for others or when we give compliments, we are practicing giving, too. Even simple gestures like saying "Good morning," or "How are you?" are giving. These are acts of kindness which do not cost anything and which we are all capable of performing, and what a tremendous difference they make! They are like small seeds that grow into enormous trees that grace our communities with pleasant, cool shade. Never overlook an opportunity to give—you will have a direct encounter with affinity.

When we are supportive of those who give, we are practicing another form of giving. When we witness others acting generously, we should acknowledge the gesture with happiness in our heart, and, if possible, thank others for their kindness—even if it wasn't directly intended for us. We should be supportive of and happy for the giver, as well as for the recipient. This may not be as easy as it sounds. Some people have the bad habit of becoming suspicious about others' motives when they see them doing good deeds. When others are nice to them, they accuse them of false flattery or of only being kind as a means to an end. When they see others give to charity, they chide them for living beyond their means. These people also begrudge those who are benefiting from the generous act. Their jealous and shortsighted attitude causes them to see the worst in others and miss opportunities to share in the joy of giving.

Happiness is an especially wonderful gift to give to others. This may mean giving our time, sharing our expertise, or helping those in need. We tend to think of happiness as a finite entity—the more we give, the less we have for ourselves. This cannot be further from the truth. Happiness is something that grows when it is shared with others, and when we share it with others, we help affinity to flourish as well. The happiness of others makes our own happiness that much more meaningful and enjoyable. We should not be afraid to share our happiness. If we keep happiness only to ourselves, we cannot fully experience or appreciate it. In keeping happiness to ourselves, we suffocate the affinity that would naturally arise if we extended it to others. Happiness, like the Dharma, cannot be fully experienced apart from others.

When we share our moments of joy with others, we feel truly blessed. Why? The following analogy may provide some clarity. When we use the flame of one candle to light other candles, the original flame does not lose its luminosity. On the contrary, it retains its brilliance, and the light from all the candles merges into a substantial and unified glow, making the room that much brighter. The state of happiness is very much like the flame of the candle. When we share our joy with others, our joy will not be lessened. I encourage you to give happiness away

freely—you will never lack happiness or good relationships in doing so.

If we pause just for a minute, we will see that we owe
our existence to the generosity of others. We'll realize that
as we nurture our relationships through giving, we should
also be thankful for what we have. Giving and thanking
always go hand in hand. What should we be thankful for?
We should be thankful for the Buddha's teachings. We
should be thankful for our parents, who gave us life and
guidance. We should be thankful for our teachers and
elders, who have broadened our knowledge. We should be
thankful to everyone known and unknown, seen and
unseen, who has enabled us to secure our basic necessities
in life. We should also be thankful for the warm sun, fresh
air, life-giving rain, and the majestic beauty of nature.
When we consider all of the causes and conditions that are
present for us to live, we should feel quite indebted to
everything we have and everyone we encounter. We will
then regard all human beings and our connections to them
in a different light.

Highly cultivated Buddhist practitioners throughout
history share the common trait of gratitude. They recognize the interconnectedness of all beings, and their gratitude is a form of practice. One example of this that comes
to mind is Venerable Yinguang, who became a monastic at
the age of twenty-one. When he first became a monk, he
was responsible for making sure that there was enough
boiled water for drinking. When he needed to boil more
water, he had first to go into the woods to get firewood.
Many people in the Venerable's shoes would have
complained at being assigned to such a menial task. Not
only was Venerable Yinguang never bitter, however, he

was very grateful for the opportunity to live and work at the temple. We are fast becoming a nation of cynics; we concentrate on being vindictive rather than being grateful. If we develop a grateful attitude, I can assure you that conflict, jealousy, and squabbles among people will be replaced with profound joy and deep affinity. Our very lives are the nourishment that affinity requires to fully manifest itself.

To remind ourselves: The other three virtues are speaking with kind words, conducting oneself for the benefit of others, and adapting oneself to others.

To practice the second virtue regarding amiable speech, we should compliment rather than reprehend others, encourage them rather than criticize, and use loving words rather than scathing remarks. Many arguments and fights have been started by an unkind utterance that could have easily remained unspoken or been replaced with gentle words instead. What was once a peaceful community can degenerate very quickly into a feuding community if lies, slander, and gossip spread among its inhabitants. If we are not paying attention, our careless words can destroy relationships. If we are mindful in our speech, being cautious always to speak with affection, our relationships will be grounded in trust and compassion.

The third virtue, conducting oneself for the benefit of others, is about always doing your best to help others. According to the Mahayana teachings, the bodhisattva spirit teaches us to put others ahead of ourselves. The bodhisattva motto is one of "wishing all sentient beings to be free of suffering." When Amitabha Buddha was still a bodhisattva, he pledged forty-eight great vows that served to guide all beings toward Buddhahood and rebirth in the World of Ultimate Bliss. Similarly, the compassion of Ksitigarbha Bodhisattva is summed up by his famous words, "As long as there is any being in hell, I vow not to become a Buddha." Bodhisattvas demonstrate the pure, altruistic spirit of putting the welfare of others ahead of oneself. If all beings practiced with this attitude, every relationship would be filled with goodness and every person would naturally and constantly strive to be of service to others. The world would be a different place if more people acted in this manner, always conducting themselves in the bodhisattva spirit.

When choosing how to conduct ourselves, there are four kinds of activities to consider, each with different levels of benefit and varying abilities to engender affinity. First are the activities that benefit others but not ourselves; second are the activities that benefit ourselves but not others; third are the activities that benefit neither others nor ourselves; and fourth are the activities that benefit others as well as ourselves. The first kind of activity, which benefits others but not ourselves, is most altruistic, and most people choose to avoid it because they are not interested in helping others simply for the sake of providing a service; they expect to receive something in return. In the *Jataka Tales*, we read of various incidents in which the Buddha, in his previous lives, helped others despite the fact that his service sometimes caused him harm. Once, in trying to rescue a pigeon from the talons of a hungry hawk, he cut off a piece of his flesh to provide the preying bird with a meal. In another lifetime, he offered himself as food to a starving mother tigress so that she might have the strength to nurse her newborn cubs.

The second kind of activity, which benefits ourselves but not others, is most prevalent, for we habitually only think of ourselves, forgetting that serving others is the most noble and gracious way to behave. How many times have we cut in line because we are in a hurry? Many of us dispose of toxic chemicals by just pouring them into a storm drain, killing all kinds of fish in the sea. Even simple acts like making a lot of noise and disturbing the peace are also reflections of our subconscious tendency to neglect the happiness and well-being of others. This kind of conduct only serves as a hindrance to building positive relationships.

The third kind of activity, which benefits neither ourselves nor others, is the most foolish, but many of us do this all the time without giving it much thought. Smoking is one of the most obvious examples of this kind of behavior. This type of conduct also includes violating the precepts, which instruct us to refrain from killing, stealing, lying, engaging in sexual misconduct, and becoming intoxicated. This kind of behavior is best avoided in our pursuit to conduct ourselves for the benefit of all beings.

The fourth kind of activity benefits others as well as ourselves. While this seems an obvious choice of action, many of us still choose to act otherwise. Let me share with you two stories of how we can benefit others as well as ourselves.

Once there was a very poor man who had nothing but a penny. He took his penny to the store to buy a piece of bread for his elderly mother. But when he arrived at the store, the storekeeper took one look at the penny and refused to sell him anything, for his penny was actually counterfeit. The poor man was heartbroken and at a loss as to what to do. Just then, a soldier passed by and asked what was troubling him. After the soldier listened to the poor man's dilemma, compassion arose in him, and he gave the man a real penny in exchange for the counterfeit one. He put the fake coin in his pocket and continued on his way to report to duty. Later, while serving on the front lines, he was hit by a bullet. Stunned by the impact, the soldier fell to the ground, but soon realized that, miraculously, he had not been hurt. As he felt his body to make sure he was not dreaming, he pulled out the counterfeit coin from his pocket. The coin, with a huge indentation in the middle, had taken the bullet for him and saved his life. His compassionate act of saving the poor man had also saved himself. At the time, he had no idea that his small, compassionate act would have such a monumental outcome, but still, he did not hesitate to help the desperate man.

Because of our habitual self-interest and our need for immediate gratification, we typically bypass opportunities to help others when we do not perceive that there will be a reward in return. Unfortunately, we often lead our lives with an attitude of, "What's in it for me?" In this way, we shortchange ourselves without even realizing it. This is one example of an action that benefits others as well as the person engaged in the action. Consider the second story:

There once was a virtuous Indian king named Sarva-datta.[1] He was a compassionate leader and would go to great lengths to help anyone in need; he shared a great affinity with his people. His reputation for kindness was well known throughout the region. In the neighboring country was a family of Brahmans. The father of the family had just passed away, leaving behind the mother, a daughter, and a young boy. Without the father, the family fell on hard times, and the mother decided to send her son to King Sarvadatta to seek his help.

At that time, King Sarvadatta's country was under attack by the greedy, tyrannical ruler of a nearby kingdom. While the king's imperial court worried about the impending attack, the king was amazingly calm and went about his day as if nothing was going on. The next day, the tyrant's army arrived outside the city gates and proceeded to march right into the city, without any opposition. It turned out that King Sarvadatta had decided to give up his kingdom so that the lives of his people would not be lost in bloodshed. Earlier in the night, the king had slipped out of the palace after leaving a written message to the tyrant, pleading with him to spare the lives of his beloved people.

The tyrant was not only a ruthless warrior, he was also a suspicious man. He feared that the king might some day return to take revenge. In order to secure his place as the new king, he let it be known that there would be a huge reward for anyone who could bring him the head of the now exiled king.

The exiled king traveled all night, securing a safe distance between himself and the tyrant, who was now sitting on the throne and ruling with a merciless heart. In his flight, the king ran into the young Brahman boy who had lost his father, and the two exchanged stories. The king took pity on the young boy and promised to help him in whatever way he could. The boy wondered how the king, who had nothing with him, could really help him. The king guessed the boy's thoughts and told him, "The tyrant may have my kingdom, but still I may be able to help you. He has promised a huge reward to anyone who brings him my head. So, if you kill me now, you can go and collect the reward." The young boy had no intention of killing the king, so the king told the boy to tie him up and take him back to the tyrant. After pondering the king's plan for a moment, the young boy did as the king suggested.

When the boy brought the king back to the city, the people were saddened to see Sarvadatta all tied up. News of the return of the king soon reached the tyrant, who ordered Sarvadatta to be brought before him. When the imperial court saw the state of Sarvadatta, they were overcome with grief. Their cries were so full of sadness that even the tyrant was moved to ask, "What are you all crying about?"

"Your Majesty, we ask for your forgiveness. We cry because we are so moved by the generous heart before us. First, he gave up his kingdom to spare the lives of his people. Now, he came back to give up his life so that he might help this young boy. He was once a king, but he did not mind being treated like a criminal. We are all moved by his kindness and benevolence."

When the tyrant heard this, he began to see why his people loved Sarvadatta so much. He went up to Sarvadatta, untied him, and handed him back his imperial seal. He told Sarvadatta, "I have your land, but it is obvious that I can never have the hearts of your people. I may as well return your land back to you."

In this way, the king got his kingdom back. In helping his people and the young boy, the king also helped himself. He was willing to part with his own life for the sake of this young boy who was a stranger to him, and for the sake of his people, with whom he had an extraordinary affinity. It is noble to care for others in spite of the fact that we may not see any perceivable benefit for ourselves. In caring for others, there are unimaginable and unexpected rewards that unfold, as in the case of the soldier and the king. By always acting in the best interest of others, we are sowing the seeds for relationships that are based on compassion and selflessness. As long as we use love to help others, our efforts are never wasted.

In striving to conduct ourselves for the benefit of others, we should model ourselves after the Buddha. The Buddha is always compassionate. Without fail and without hesitation, he puts the welfare of others before his own. He is a good example of what we mean by, "Be the first to worry about the world's problems, be the last to enjoy its prosperity." Instead of thinking, "What can others do for me?" we should think, "What can I do for others?" President John Fitzgerald Kennedy of the United States once stated in a very famous speech, "Ask not what your country can do for you; ask what you can do for your country." His presidential platform sought to bring harmony and unity to our country. If we can bear this idea in mind, we can participate in bringing harmony and unity to our relationships.

The fourth virtue, adapting oneself to others, tells us to put ourselves in others' shoes. If we try to force our own agenda, without taking the other person's experience or state of mind into consideration, we are not being respectful. Worse yet, if we judge others' points of view as inferior to our own, we are being counterproductive to creating good relationships; we are compromising the spirit of affinity. We should regard others' point of view with utmost respect and try to understand where they are coming from, even if we do not agree with them. When we are sincere with others and don't simply dismiss their viewpoint because it differs from our own or seems unimportant in our eyes, relationships have a better chance of flourishing into something positive and trusting, and everything just seems to fall into place.

If we are successful in being sympathetic to another's perspective, we will not be so quick to lay blame at others' feet or so stubborn in asserting our own opinion. By practicing this virtue, many potential arguments will simply not come to fruition. The following story demonstrates how a certain family has not yet put the fourth great virtue into practice. As each family member maintains his own rigid viewpoint without considering the other's feelings, an argument escalates that could have easily been avoided.

It was a hot day; Lee decided to turn on the fan. Chan was annoyed and yelled, "Don't just think about yourself. You know I have a cold. Please turn off the fan."

Chan's yelling kindled Lee's anger, and he answered back, "You are the one with the cold. If you don't like the fan, you can sit over there."

Now, Lee was really angry and shot back, "Why should I move?"

One wants to turn on the fan, and the other wants it off. One is hot, while the other has a cold. When they only take their own comfort into consideration, instead of trying to be thoughtful and considerate about the other person's feelings, a difficult situation ensues. What if Chan had put himself in Lee's shoes from the beginning and simply moved out of the way of the fan so Lee could be cool? Or, what if Lee had just apologized to Chan for pointing the fan in his direction and simply moved the fan so it blew elsewhere? If they had only considered the other's point of view and made minor adjustments, the whole incident would have just blown over. In this way, affinity is energized, not stifled; peaceful coexistence is nurtured, not arrested.

Another way to practice the virtue of adapting ourselves to others is through a simple method that we can use in our everyday life. When practiced sincerely and without resentment, this method works every time. All you have to do is remember this: "You are right; I am wrong." This may sound counterintuitive because we are so entrenched in our habit of looking out for ourselves and defending our own opinions; however, it is a worthwhile practice and always keeps peace between people. I encourage you to try "You are right and I am wrong"— even if only once. Your affinity with others will bloom like a lovely flower, and potential conflicts will wither away.

When we practice the four great all-embracing virtues, we are on our way to realizing our capacity for connection with others. Taking is turned into giving, harsh words are turned into compassionate ones, selfish thinking is turned into consideration for others, troublesome relationships are turned into harmonious ones, and animosity is turned into affinity.

The six points of reverent harmony

Social harmony stems from handling relationships and communal living with skill, effort, and a spirit of cooperation. We can learn a lot about keeping peace in social living from the six points of reverent harmony that the monastic sangha observes. *Sangha* is a Sanskrit word that can be interpreted on many different levels. In its widest interpretation, it refers to all those who have the common purpose of following the Dharma. The six points of harmony, or unity, in Buddhist monastic life are: doctrinal unity in views, economic unity in communal use of goods, moral unity through upholding the precepts, mental unity through shared joy, verbal unity through loving speech and refraining from criticisms and discord, and physical unity by living harmoniously in the same community.

Harmony in views: In the monastic sangha, monks and nuns share a common view of the Dharma, the guiding principle for all they do. Similarly, a society has a better chance to prosper when its people share common political and social views. If we look at the different nations of the world, we notice that there is a lot more cooperation and common ground in prosperous nations than in those that are less prosperous.

Harmony in economics: In the monastic sangha, all renunciants live an equally simple life and have equal access to the communal property. In the secular world, a society is inherently unstable if there is too much of a disparity between the haves and the have-nots. Also, the less effort invested in creating affinity, the wider the gap is between the rich and the poor. Thus, those who are well off should help those who are less fortunate. Those who are able should help those who are not.

Harmony in morality: In the monastic sangha, all individuals share the same moral code. In society, everyone should be equal in the eyes of the law. No one should be above the law. When the law is equally and justly applied to all, people will have respect for the law and will be more inclined to abide by it.

Harmony in outlook: In the monastic sangha, all share the common purpose of spiritual development. In society, when we have concern for others' well-being, we accept

others and are not envious of their success or critical of
their shortcomings. We seek to uplift our fellow citizens,
instead of oppressing them. Equanimity, support, and
affirmation provide the foundation for peaceful living.
With harmony in outlook, every place is a pure land.

Harmony in speech: In the monastic sangha, monks and
nuns practice loving speech, and refrain from criticisms
and discord. This practice fosters harmony in their
community. In society, misunderstandings and animosity
often arise from unskillful or harsh words. Therefore,
being sincere and thoughtful in our speech can often lead
to harmonious human relationships.

Harmony in deeds: In the monastic sangha, monks and
nuns bodily observe the same rites and rituals. In society,
our actions can be used to help each other and foster
respect in the world. In this way, we can peacefully coexist
in the community.

These six points of harmony are as applicable to lay
people as they are to monastics. Much societal discord
could be transformed into societal accord if all members of
a community took these observances to heart. If every
single person could simply uphold "Harmony in speech,"
then even in the presence of opposing political, economic,
or moral positions, many feuds and brutalities would never
come into being. When we integrate the Buddha's teachings into daily life, then the true beauty of relationships is
revealed to us. We will directly experience the fact that
affinity sings and discord grumbles.

Grounding relationships in oneness
Harmony and beauty within our lives and within our
communities often fail due to our insistence on the duality

of self and others. The ultimate solution for generating peace and accord in our relationships and in our world, therefore, lies in seeing that we all are one. Never-Disparaging Bodhisattva[2] was always respectful to everyone he met, for he knew that we are all capable of becoming a Buddha one day. He did not maintain a dual, and therefore erroneous, perception that distinguished between people he deemed worthy of being treated with esteem and people he deemed unworthy. Through recognizing the interconnectedness of all beings, the perceived distance between all beings will shrink and an affirming environment will grow. If we all practice a modicum of this kind of regard for others, the world will be a much better place.

When we maintain the duality of self and others, we develop disproportionate levels of love and hatred, attraction and repulsion for other people, which throws our relationships out of balance; the capacity for affinity becomes dormant. We judge everyone around us, putting people into categories such as good and bad, acceptable and unacceptable, worthy and unworthy. We want to spend time with those whom we love and accept, and we avoid socializing with those whom we dislike. Clinging to the notion of self and others causes these discriminating mindsets, and they disrupt the harmony and balance within a community. If we replace this spirit of separateness with compassion, much of the friction in human relations will disappear. If we realize that we all are one, then there will be no impulse to jealousy and no room for conflict. There will be no inclination to like or dislike people; everyone will be regarded with the eyes of compassion. Through the eyes of oneness, we are never tempted to say that one group, or one person, is more important or more valuable than the other. The *Diamond Sutra* teaches us that there is no boundary or chasm that separates self and others, and that we should seek to let go of this mental construct. Dissolving our dualistic world-view creates an environment in which natural affinity arises. When we can practice viewing ourselves and others through a lens of oneness, we will no longer engage in meaningless mind games that prevent us from forming positive connections with all beings.

Each of us, like a fine strand in a web, is a part of the overall picture. Take a look at the five fingers of the hand. They are all different in length. Without these differences, we will not have the dexterity that we take for granted. Each finger by itself cannot exert much force. However, if we combine the force of the five fingers, say into a fist, we can really pack a punch. Celebrating the differences in people while viewing everyone through the eyes of oneness nurtures powerful connections and creates a plane of existence where everyone is mutually supportive and respectful.

People from all walks of life, with different interests and inclinations, need to remember this sense of coopera-tion, including Buddhist practitioners from various schools. From one temple to another, from monastics to laity, we should embrace each other wholeheartedly. Regardless of whether we are of the Chan School, Pure Land School, or Tantric School, we are all followers of the Buddha, and, as such, we deserve mutual respect. As long as we are supporting the purpose of the sangha, it does not matter what color our skin is or what school we follow. Under the umbrella of Buddhism, we all share a common teacher, the Buddha. With equanimity, we all should support each other in our common goal of spreading the Dharma. With open hearts and non-discriminating minds, we will be "seeking the Dharma in the people," and like Never-Disparaging Bodhisattva we will recognize the Buddha in every person.

Throughout history, we see that the differentiation of *us* versus *them* is the cause of many conflicts and wars. The Holocaust is one of the ugliest examples of such differentiation. Likewise, in the Balkans, the atrocity of ethnic cleansing was the cause of many large-scale tragedies. Instead of rejecting those who are different from us, we should learn to embrace them. The peace and harmony that ensue from mutual respect and acceptance make the initial efforts all worthwhile. Instead of accentuating our differences, we should highlight our similarities. While we may look or act differently, we are fundamentally alike. After all, it is because we share similar causes and conditions that we were reborn in this world at this time. All beings share an inherent connection, and we can either embrace or deny this, living in a manner that draws this out or leaves it dormant. We should treasure the similar conditions that bring us together as neighbors, friends, and fellow inhabitants of this precious world.

Bodhisattvas embody this spirit of fundamental similarity and oneness. They love all sentient beings as if they were their own sons and daughters; they see no beings as separate from themselves. When we suffer, they feel our pain; when we celebrate, they feel our joy. In the eyes of the bodhisattvas, we are intimately related to them. When they help us, they are also helping themselves. This is what is meant when we say, "Cultivate loving-kindness without conditions and ground compassion in oneness." Thus, if we want to awaken our true capacity for happiness, we have to first take down the walls that separate us from each other. This is part of recognizing, affirming, and strengthening the interlocking web of human relationships of which we are all a part.

The Sixth Patriarch of the Chan School of Buddhism once said, "The Dharma is in the world; enlightenment cannot be realized apart from the world. Seeking bodhi apart from the world is like looking for horns on a rabbit." From this, we see that the Dharma is in the world, in every one of us. If we want to experience the Dharma, we should first start by understanding that we all are one. When our view of the world is grounded in oneness, then our lives will be truly joyous and meaningful.

I have personally experienced how much better life can be when it is grounded in oneness. In my early years, I came into some money from the books and articles I had authored. Using this money, I purchased a fairly nice house, thinking that it would give me a place to concentrate on my writing. True, the house was comfortable, but I wanted to extend comfort to all people, so I ended up selling it and using the proceeds to start Fo Guang Shan. Now, when I hear the voices of young students reciting their lessons at the schools of Fo Guang Shan or when I see devotees coming to pay their respects to the Buddha, I feel immense joy. Even though I personally do not possess anything, the gift of seeing how Fo Guang Shan has blossomed is many times greater than the comfort of living in a nice house. When we look at this world through the eyes of the community, we will never lack affinity with others.

Huineng (who later became the Sixth Patriarch of the Chan School) speaks of oneness well in his first encounter with the Fifth Patriarch of the Chan School. Huineng was a woodcutter before he joined the monastics. When Huineng first met the Fifth Patriarch, he told the Patriarch that he had traveled a long way to learn the Buddha's teachings. The Patriarch asked him, "Where do you come from?"

"I come from Lingnan," answered Huineng.

The Fifth Patriarch wanted to test him further, "Lingnan is a place of barbarians and uncivilized people. Surely they do not have Buddha-nature."

To which Huineng replied, "People can be classified as northerners or southerners, but everyone shares the same Buddha-nature."

When we go beyond our external differences, we will realize they are but temporary shrouds that cover our true nature. We will know that we are all the same and have the same Buddha-nature. In this way, the perceived distance between people is decreased and the chasm is crossed. When we remember that we are all of the same nature, then we will see there is no reason why we cannot live together in harmony.

✑ CHAPTER TWO ✑

A Closer Look at Relationships
Affinity in Friendship, Emotions, and Love

AMONG OUR MANY RELATIONSHIPS, many forms and types exist. There are friendships, family connections, teacher-student bonds, marriages, relationships with and between monastics, and many other kinds. How we choose to develop, nourish, and manage these specific relationships determines our own joy and contentment, as well as that of our fellow human beings and, ultimately, our community and world as a whole. How wonderful our lives become when we trust in the infinite and inherent capacity for connection that all beings share. Living with utmost ease and happiness and with the maximum ability to benefit others depends on our ability and willingness to approach all relationships with compassion, pure hearts, and the proper frame of mind. Consider the following example.

Once there was a man who asked a Chan master to write something special for his birthday. The Chan master wrote, "Father expires, son expires, grandson expires." The man was not at all amused by the mentioning of death on his birthday. The Chan master explained, "These are words of good luck."

The man was puzzled. "Everyone dies. What kind of good luck is this?" he asked.

The Chan master replied, "Would you rather have your grandson pass away before your son and before you? How tragic it is to have elders attending the funerals of the young!"

When we do not have a clear understanding of how we relate to others, or how we *can* relate to others, we create a lot of unnecessary problems for ourselves and others. We miss out on the great joy that is easily within our reach. Therefore, it is important for us to nurture our skills in developing and maintaining various types of relationships so we can heighten our ability to offer compassion and love that serves to empower and elevate others, rather than suppress or oppress them.

There are many instances in which the sutras speak of how relationships should be handled. These texts guide us in eliminating the distance between people and help us to nurture profound affinity. While there are historical and cultural differences in how any relationship is best managed, the basic elements of respect and compassion are the universal ingredients of a good and healthy relationship. Here we will look specifically at what the sutras say regarding friendships, and then discuss healthy emotions and love. Taking these teachings and suggestions to heart can help us all generate widespread and long-lasting affinity with our fellow sentient beings.

Friendship
According to the sutras, there are four kinds of friends: friends who treat you like a flower, friends who act like a balance, friends who are like the mountains, and friends who are like the earth.

We all enjoy flowers, especially when they are fresh. We put them in vases to decorate our homes, we give them to our loved ones to express our affection, and we may even wear them in our hair. However, when the flowers wilt, we toss them out like trash. Some people treat their friends like this. They are delighted as long as their friends can fulfill certain needs of theirs, but when their friends outlive their usefulness, they toss them out like wilted flowers. When their friends are prosperous and thriving, they treat them with reverence. When their friends are down on their luck or losing their vitality, they distance themselves from their friends and their misfortune. This can be seen in the saying, "The poor live in the city without anyone asking after them. The rich live in secluded areas and distant relatives come calling." It is so habitual for us to love what is beautiful and scorn what is not. Curbing this tendency is a significant step in making and maintaining friendships that will last a lifetime.

There are, then, some people who act like a scale and continually compare themselves to their friends. They are envious when they perceive their friends to be doing better than they are, and are boastful when they feel like the scale is tipping in their own direction. The scale will never be balanced, for these people are not content unless they have "one-upped" their friends. This kind of judging and comparing within a friendship is quite damaging.

Some friends are analogous to mountains. Like mountains that are full of rich ore, flowers and wildlife, these friends are full of treasures and wonders. With these friends, we are constantly reminded of the beauty and diversity of life. We can learn a lot in these friendships.

Some friends are like the great earth that lets everything grow in its rich soil. Such friends can help us grow in our wisdom and strengthen our character.

The *Agamas* speak of the four kinds of friends that should be cultivated. The first kind is friends that can help us tell right from wrong. They let us know when our conduct is admirable and are not afraid to tell us when we behave poorly. Such friends help us stay on the right path. The second kind is friends that are compassionate and caring. They give us moral support during our trying times. They are also happy for us when we are doing well. The third kind is friends that are always ready to extend a helping hand. They are pillars of strength. They help us stay focused and come to our aid when we are lost. The fourth kind is friends that share our aspirations. Such friends provide us with encouragement and are not hesitant to share their time and resources. Good friends can help us discover our capacity for connection. When we cultivate these relationships properly, we will be experts at living affinity.

The sutras also speak of the five types of friends that we should avoid. The first type is friends that never show their true intentions. These people are not trustworthy or sincere and take advantage of others with no remorse. The second type is friends that are envious of others' good fortune and success. They constantly wallow in bitterness and resentment. The third type is friends that have hearts of stone. They only think about themselves and fail to see or care about others' predicaments. The fourth type is friends that do not acknowledge their own mistakes. They are quick to place blame on others, instead of being willing to learn and grow from their own foolish conduct. The fifth type is friends that refuse to accept advice from others. Their minds are closed and their character is arrogant. Although we should still show kindness and compassion to all of these people, it is not wise to keep their company. Friendships should be based on mutual affinity, not one-sided effort. Real friendships are an actual and resounding expression of true joy.

In addition to friendships, the sutras also address other human relationships such as those between spouses, parents and their children, monastics, or people of different social standing. The Buddha's teachings are full of guidance on building affinity with others, for how we relate to people is the foundation of any kind of practice and of a peaceful and cooperative coexistence. Our capacity to create and nurture affinity is infinite; we simply need to uncover the wisdom and motivation to do so.

A key element for us as we strive to relate to each other in more appropriate and expansive ways is the way we regard and manage our emotions. No relationship is barren of emotions, and it is essential that they be investigated and handled with wisdom. I wish to explore emotions in the following pages, with hope that we can all handle our relationships with increased skill, so that all beings can benefit from our ever-expanding ability to love.

Healthy emotions, healthy love

Our emotions are a very important part of our everyday life, and they play a leading role on the stage of relationships. The ability to feel and the freedom to act upon these feelings give us both joy and sorrow, and it is imperative that we maintain our emotional well-being to minimize the potential for suffering within relationships. Emotions are the glue that binds relationships together, and, remember, relationships form the basis of society. In other words, the human experience is comprised of relationships, and relationships are comprised of emotions. Therefore, a stable, positive, supportive, and healthy community depends upon stable, positive, supportive, and healthy emotions. Many people make the mistake of thinking that the Buddha's teachings disapprove of emotions. This is far from the truth. Buddhism does not encourage people to shed their emotions, but teaches us how to lead a healthy emotional life by not becoming attached to them or controlled by them. How do we ensure that our emotional states remain healthy? In this regard, the Buddha teaches us to use compassion to channel our emotions and to use wisdom to guide the unbridled forces of our emotions. While we often think of the Buddha as the fully enlightened one, we should not forget that he was also a most affectionate and loving human being. The Buddha certainly experienced emotions, but he did so without any attachment to them; they had no power to overwhelm him or control his behavior.

None of us can live in an emotional vacuum; all of us participate in a variety of relationships where we experience many different kinds of emotions. For instance, the strength and character of emotions that exist between a husband and a wife are different from those between a father and son, between siblings, or between friends. However, in all relationships, love and affection are the common denominator. For this reason, while exploring healthy emotions, we will focus mainly on the emotion of love, examining potential problems that arise from misguided love, as well as the incredible potential of love to liberate all beings. We will see that love can help us reveal our true potential for living affinity.

Very often, we hear people raise this question: "Where do we come from?" The sutras tell us that we human beings arise out of love; in fact, it is said in the sutras, "When one's love is not strong, one will not be born into the *Saha* world." Love is the source of life, and our existence represents a continuum of love and affection. We are walking, talking, breathing, and learning manifestations of love, and our capacity to give it away is boundless.

While some kinds of love are "healthy," others are "unhealthy"; some are "giving," others are "possessive." Love has its pluses and minuses. From the perspective of its pluses, love gives us the strength to make sacrifices, to give, to encourage, to connect and to be compassionate. Love is like a road map: it gives our lives direction and we can see our destination with clear visibility. Love is like a blanket: it provides us with warmth and security. Love is like a box of chocolates: it is sweet and full of surprises. From the perspective of its minuses, love is like a piece of rope: it can be binding and restrictive. Love is like a lock: it can shackle us and make us restless. Love can be blinding: it can keep us in the dark without any awareness that we have compromised our principles and standards. Love is like the honey on a sharp blade: it can entice us to lick the blade, even at the risk of cutting our tongues and risking our lives. Love can be like a sea of suffering: its turbulent waves can trap us in its depths.

We all want to be loved. Some people move beyond only wanting to receive love, and they devote their lives to sharing their love with others. Regardless of whether we love or are loved by others, we have to be watchful that our love does not turn sour. Love and hate are inseparable, one shadowing the other. If we do not love properly, and if we do not expand our love for a few to compassion for all, love will remain small and powerless in helping all beings live with happiness and freedom. And pristine love is anything but small and powerless—it is the reason for our existence!

Ending with the Buddha as the most shining example of love, I would like to discuss four different levels of love and affection, and to offer some insight on how to nurture them in healthy and positive ways. We will progress from basic love to transcendental love. You may recognize yourself in one or more of these levels, but we can all have faith that we contain within us the inherent ability to love at the highest possible level. The various levels are the stepping-stones toward developing relationships that are affirming and liberating, ultimately resulting in the creation of a peaceful and harmonious existence where affinity is beautifully actualized.

Different levels of love and affection
1. Everyday Love: Everyday love is the first level of love. It is the most basic and common form of affinity. This includes love between a man and a woman, between a parent and a child, among family members, and between friends. While everyday love can be blissful, there are

times when love can hurt. While most of us know or long for the joys of love, we may not understand why love can cause us so much pain. Because of this, I believe it is more useful if we spend some time examining this pain. There are three main situations when love causes us problems:

(i) When the object of our love is inappropriate
It is human nature to love someone with whom we feel a special bond. However, when the object of our love is inappropriate, our love can keep us in a constant state of disappointment and turmoil. When we love someone who is spoken for or is married to another person, our love is destined for trouble. It takes two to love; when we love someone who has no feeling for us, it is like banging our head against the wall. Depending on the object of our love, we should also moderate our intensity accordingly. If not, problems will ensue and, instead of helping, we will harm ourselves and others.

(ii) When our perspective of love is inappropriate
One of the most common, though faulty, perspectives of love is to view love as some kind of acquisition. Some people believe that, because of their personal wealth, they can buy love. Others dare not love others who are more affluent than they are because they do not feel worthy to do so. Other people would not consider falling in love with someone without first considering that person's looks, education, profession, social status or how wealthy his or her family is. In these instances, love is looked at as a kind of trade, one in which a person's main motivation in loving another is to gain something. Love is a quest for status, reputation, money, or other temporary forms of security.

This is an erroneous perspective on love and a devastating mockery of its potential. True love does not speak of requirements and prerequisites; true love is about giving.

(iii) When the manner in which we love is inappropriate
Some people only love themselves and have little regard for others; their love is egocentric in nature. They are in continual pursuit of personal enjoyment, not caring if they hurt others in the process. Others let their own emotions cloud their judgment; they become partial to people they love and overly critical of those whom they dislike. Sometimes, love is like a pair of colored glasses, preventing us from seeing the true face of those we love and keeping us in an unhealthy and perpetual state of denial. No wonder we say that love is blind. There is a common Chinese saying that we can use as our guide, "Know the ills of those we love and the goodness of those we dislike." When we love properly, love brings out the best in each one of us.

When we love improperly, our affection for others can be obsessive. When we love someone, we feel we have a special claim on him or her. In Chinese literature, the desire to possess exclusively those whom we love is often compared to the intolerance of the human eye. Eyes are very sensitive and reject even the tiniest grain of sand. Likewise, in love we have the tendency to reject even the smallest encroachments on our relationships. This desire is almost instinctive; even a three-year-old toddler can be possessive of his or her mother. True love, however, is not about possession, but about giving. Relationships that are built on the desire to possess are doomed to failure, for sooner or later the urge to possess will degenerate into jealousy or become an insatiable demand for more and more of the other person. Subduing the urge to possess and increasing the motivation to give strengthens all relationships, including marital relationships.

Let me clarify what I mean with the following experience I had. Among the devotees of a particular temple was a lady whose husband was a very successful businessman. One day she found out, to her dismay, that her husband had a mistress. Feeling betrayed, she became angry and began to ignore her husband. She gave her husband the cold shoulder, and whatever conversations they had inevitably escalated into a fight. Sensing her hostility and experiencing an increasingly cold and unwelcome environment, the husband became even more reluctant to spend time at home. The marriage seemed to be beyond salvation.

One day, the lady came to me and tearfully told me her situation. She wanted me to counsel her as to what she should do. I told her, "I know of a way to win his heart back and heal your marriage, but I am not sure if you are willing to give it a try."

"I will do whatever you tell me to. Please."

I explained to her, "First of all, you have to let go of your angry and hateful attitude, and realize that nothing has happened that cannot be forgiven and repaired. I suggest treating your husband with the same kindness and affection that you would have done if he had not made such a terrible mistake. If you confront your husband directly, it will only drive him farther away from you. Accusations and angry criticisms are not the path toward reconciliation. Second, when your husband comes home from work, I want you to really try to understand where he is coming from. When he realizes that he can find warmth and love at home, he himself will come to the conclusion that there is no need for him to have an affair. Only love can win back love."

The wife did exactly as I instructed her. Before long, her husband had a change of heart and stopped his harmful behavior. As it turned out, she was also partly responsible for the problems in their marriage. She understood that she was often an overly demanding and nagging wife. Her overbearing personality gave her husband an excuse to look for "happiness" outside the home. They realized that they both had a role to play in the loss of the caring and nurturing atmosphere of their marriage.

After my conversation with her, both the man and woman sensed a genuine change in each other and once more felt loved in their own home. One day, the husband asked his wife, "What has changed in you? You seem like a different person." When she told him of our conversation, he was very thankful that her religion had played a role in saving their marriage, and he, too, began to visit the temple regularly.

This may be just one anecdote, and it may not be the panacea for all marital problems. It does, however, help to illustrate the fact that hatred cannot win love. Only when there is open willingness to give does love have a chance to flourish. When a rift develops between a couple, if just one party is willing to give a little extra, there is hope. Within a relationship, giving begets more giving; it is contagious. If both parties refuse to give, even a small squabble may spiral out of control. In a relationship, the desire to control the other party will only serve to snuff out the life of a relationship. It is unfortunate when love becomes the cause of problems and heartbreaks. When I read in the newspaper about the many alarming stories of love-driven assaults or even homicides, I cannot help but lament how tragic it is not to love properly. Giving is the best nutrient that helps relationships grow. Relationships that are grounded in mutual giving are always trusting and happy ones. The shared affinity in these types of relationships creates a kind of positive energy that influences all of our other relationships, strengthening and deepening their connections.

Even if we cannot constantly give to our loved ones and make huge sacrifices for them, the least we can do is not to hurt them. In the *Documentary of the Warring Period*, Yue Yi[3] once said, "When a gentleman breaks off a friendship, he does not speak ill of the other party. When a patriotic official is asked to leave the emperor's court, he does not try to clear his name." Similarly, while most people would like to see their romance develop into marital bliss, it is important to know how to handle a relationship when it fails. When friends part ways, they should do so amiably and not bear a grudge. How can one make an enemy out of someone whom one has once loved? To defame or destroy another person just because of a failed relationship is so unnecessary. We must learn how to both love and cope with failed love in an appropriate manner.

(iv) When our attachment to love is inappropriate

We all should treasure our relationships with our family and friends. Without the necessary causes and conditions, we would not have been brought together. While we treasure our relationships, we should not become overly attached to them, either. All of us, at one point or another, will experience the pain of separation. Separation from our loved ones is one of the eight sufferings we all have to endure, whether it's from growing up, physical distance, choosing a lifestyle apart from the family, death, or other reasons. *The Way to Buddhahood* by Venerable Yin-shun states, "Those with fame and high status can still fall. Those who are together may be scattered." The manner in which we handle such a devastating situation is very important, for it influences our internal and external environment and influences how we approach other relationships.

I still remember some twenty years ago, when Venerable Tzu Chuang decided to renounce the household life to become a monastic, and her parents came to witness the ordination ceremony. With tears in their eyes, they gave her a warm smile. Why were they both happy and sad? Although it is quite common now for young college graduates to enter the monastic life, it was quite unusual at that time. On the one hand, Tzu Chuang's parents wanted to spend the rest of their lives with their child; on the other hand, they recognized their daughter's love and dedication to the Dharma. Their tears, as well as their smiles, left a strong impression in my memory. The parents are powerful examples of individuals transforming the desire to possess into the joy of giving, and of handling separation with dignity and altruism.

There are a few things we can do to help us cope with changes and separation in our relationships. We should have a variety of interests to keep us busy so that we do not have to measure our happiness by how often we are able to spend time with those we love. When our relationships with our friends and family change, we can build new relationships, too. If we expand our own individual support circle, then we are less inclined to be demanding of a particular person's time and attention. Last but not least, we should find happiness within ourselves and not in external elements. In doing so, we will find lasting contentment in spite of all of the changes and separations we experience; we will not be so thrown by life's impermanence. If we are too attached to our relationships, we will only know suffering when what we once had fades or disappears.

What happens when our loved ones die and leave us forever? Let me share this account from a sutra with you. During the time of the Buddha, there was an elderly woman with an only son. She loved her son dearly and had always hoped that he would look after her when she became old and dependent. Unfortunately, her son fell ill one day and died shortly thereafter. The woman was beside herself with anguish. Grief-stricken, she carried the body to where the Buddha was staying in the hope that he could bring her son back to life. The Blessed One took pity on her and said, "If you want me to bring your son back to life, there is a way. You have to first bring me a small mustard seed, and not just any mustard seed. This mustard seed must come from a house that has not known death." With hope, the mother went from house to house, trying to find one where no one had died. Everywhere she went, someone in the family had once passed away. She searched in vain, and finally, after knocking on all the doors, went back to the Buddha and told him what happened. The Buddha gently explained, "From time immemorial, humankind has lived and died. Such is the law of nature. You should not be overwrought with your son's death." The elderly woman was enlightened.

My maternal grandmother was a very religious woman and remains a good example of treasuring relationships without being overly attached to them. She began her life-long vegetarian practice when she was seventeen, the same time she began her practice of reciting Amitabha's name. She was a very compassionate woman and had a lot of influence on my decision to join the sangha. She had three sons with families of their own, but unfortunately all their children died very young, at around three or four years of age. My grandmother was never bitter about the misfortune, and not because she did not feel the loss. She was a Buddhist in the truest sense of the word. She realized that when there is birth, there is also death, and we reap what we sow. The birth of her grandchildren was the culmination of causes and conditions; their departure, too, was the result of conditionality. The human life span is not that long to begin with, and we should not excessively grieve over the loss of our loved ones. Many of us choose to believe in the law of conditionality when things are going well for us but would question its validity when tragedy strikes. My grandmother truly knew how to put sorrows into perspective. She was an inspiration to me in my own handling of headaches and heartaches.

When there is life, there is also death; when there is union, there is also separation. We should treasure our relationships while they last and let go of them when separation becomes inevitable. This is difficult for those who believe that as love grows, so does attachment. Pure love actually points us toward a life without any attachments and helps us tread the path toward true freedom.

We have looked at various examples of everyday love and explored the qualities of healthy and unhealthy love, appropriate and inappropriate love. As we learn how to love more skillfully and expansively, our love will evolve to a higher plane. Our love will grow from everyday love into heroic love, which is quite remarkable and extraordinary.

2. Heroic Love: How is heroic love remarkable and extraordinary? How does it differ from the everyday love we talked about in the previous section? I am going to give a few examples here to help us answer these questions.

(i) Selfless love for your country
Dayu was a well-known virtuous man of ancient China. During that time, there was a major flood, and many people lost their farms and homes. The emperor assigned Dayu to see what could be done to divert the river water and alleviate the floods. Dayu was away from home for thirteen years, supervising the project. He was so dedicated to finishing the project and thus relieving his fellow citizens of further pain that, during these thirteen years, he passed his house three times and did not stop to visit with his family. In his love for his country and fellow citizens, Dayu had little time for himself and his family. Although he loved and missed his family, he was willing to extend his love to his community to such a degree that he was prepared to be apart from them during this crisis. His heart was dedicated to liberating other people from misery and devastation, so much so that enduring his own pain and loneliness in order to do so was a worthwhile sacrifice. Such selfless love for one's country is a very good example of heroic love.

During the Epoch of Warring States in ancient China, there was a government official by the name of Qu Yuan. He was very patriotic and was highly trusted by King Huai of Chu State. When some of the corrupt officials began to see themselves losing ground to Qu Yuan, they began to spread false rumors about him. Unfortunately, the emperor believed the rumors and distanced himself from Qu Yuan, finally dispatching him to a faraway post. Even then, Qu Yuan loved his emperor and maintained high hopes that his country would not fall into the hands of these corrupt officials. He would rather end his life in the name of patriotism than be forced to agree to the plans of political parasites. When he was ordered by the emperor to either implement a policy put forward by the corrupt officials or face death, he chose death. He jumped into Miluo Lake[4] and took his own life. When the emperor realized what a grave mistake he had made, he launched an effort to find Qu Yuan's body. As the villagers searched for his body, they rowed around the lake in boats and made loud noises with their drums to scare the fish away. They couldn't bear the idea of fish feeding on his body. From many of the letters left behind by Qu Yuan, we can witness his steadfast love for his country. He decided that he would rather take his own life than helplessly watch his country decline. This is another example of selfless patriotic love for one's country.

During the later years of the Song Dynasty, China was divided into the Northern Song and Southern Song lands. When the poet Lu Fangweng lay on his deathbed, he told his sons, "As I lie dying, I know that all phenomena are empty; however, I grieve that I will never see the unification of the nine states. On the day the imperial army of the Song Dynasty reclaims the north, please do not forget to tell me the news when you make your ancestral offerings."

These three stories illustrate the remarkable dedication and persevering love that some people give to their country. This form of love can be considered heroic because it is more than a mere fondness for one's home and it often involves making strenuous sacrifices. To love with heroism, one must be willing to sacrifice one's own peace for the peace of others, one's own happiness for the happiness of others, and even one's own life for the lives of others.

(ii) Selfless love for others

One of the Buddha's cousins was a general by the name of Mahanama. He was responsible for guarding the city of Kapilavastu. When the city was attacked and was about to fall into the hands of its enemies, Mahanama pleaded with the opposing general, "Please do not kill my people. However, if you aren't willing to show mercy, can you please wait until I resurface after jumping down to the bottom of the river?" The other general was none other than the fierce King Virudhaka. He looked at Mahanama and answered, "As you and your people have no escape, I will grant you your last wish." Mahanama then jumped into the river and disappeared. A long time passed and he still did not float back up. Virudhaka was getting impatient and sent his people to the bottom of the river to find out what happened. They found Mahanama at the bottom of the river with his hair tied to a tree root. In giving his life, he bought some time for his people to escape from the city. This kind of willingness to sacrifice oneself for others is a form of fearless love. It is, indeed, extraordinary love.

(iii) Selfless love for the Dharma

If one is familiar with Chinese Buddhism, one has surely heard of Master Xuanzang. He is referred to as the "Confucius of Chinese Buddhism." Master Xuanzang is remembered for his determination to go to India to learn about Buddhism and for bringing sutras back to China. To do this, he had to cross over eight hundred miles of desert. One day, while he was in the desert, all of the water that he and his entourage were carrying suddenly spilled out. The situation was extremely serious, because there was little chance they could cross the desert without water. Thirsting under the fierce sun, he made this very famous vow: "I would rather die trying to take the last step westward than try to make it back east alive." This fervor for truth is a form of remarkable love.

If you examine how the Japanese live, eat, and dress, you will see that there is a heavy flavor of Chinese influence. Who was the first to introduce Chinese culture to Japan? For this, we have to credit Venerable Jianzhen of the Tang Dynasty. He was one of the earliest principal figures of the area of Yangzhou,[5] where I grew up. In order to realize his dream of going to Japan to spread the Dharma, Jianzhen tried to cross the sea to Japan on seven different occasions over a twelve-year period. One time, he was stopped by government officials; another time, he was robbed clean by bandits. On another attempt, he had to turn back because of bad weather and turbulent seas. There was even one time when he was betrayed and exposed by one of his disciples. After six difficult attempts, he finally arrived in Japan at the age of sixty, blind in both eyes. Even with all these hardships, his resolve of spreading the Dharma in Japan remained unshaken. He made this moving remark about his experience: "What is the risking of life in the face of great undertakings?" Jianzhen did not hesitate to give up his life for the opportunity to spread the Dharma. His compassionate act of spreading the truth to all demonstrated a remarkable love for others.

During the Tang Dynasty, there was a monk called Venerable Congjian. He came from the city of Nanyang and became a monk in his middle years, after he had married and had a son. For twenty years after joining the monastics, Congjian did not visit his family even once. One day, while he was working in the temple garden, a young man came up to him and asked, "Reverend monk, please tell me where I can find Venerable Congjian."

Congjian was taken by surprise and asked the young man in return, "Why are you looking for him?"

The young man replied, "The venerable is my father. I have not seen him for twenty years; I just want to pay him a visit."

Pointing to a distant corner in the garden, Congjian told the young man, "You can find your father over there," and hurried away. When the young man walked over to where Congjian had pointed, he could not find his father. By the time he discovered that the venerable he had been speaking to was, in fact, his own father, Congjian had already disappeared without a trace.

On the surface, it appeared that Congjian was a cold and emotionless man. In reality, he did not acknowledge his own son because he was afraid that his love for his son would cause him to lose his resolve to practice the Dharma for the sake of all beings. He loved his son dearly, but not in an outward or conventional way.

The famous Venerable Hongyi was also married before he joined the sangha. He, too, refused to meet with his wife when she came to visit. We cannot because of this call the venerable a heartless man. The venerable was most compassionate. He did not confine his love to his own family, but gave his love to all sentient beings. He gave himself to those who needed his help, and by teaching the Dharma he gave many people hope and direction, building affinity with every word. His contributions to spreading the Dharma were immense and definitely not the conduct of an unloving man.

While monastics view relationships with more detachment than do people in the secular world, they are no less sincere. In many temples, we find the following two-line stanza, which explains this loving yet detached form of relationship:

Mind not temple tea and rice being light;
Monastic relationships less consuming than laity's.

Monastics focus their entire lives on the transcendent; this is where their primary attention rests. Sometimes, therefore, the phenomenal world, which includes relationships, is kept somewhat at a distance so that the monastics' spiritual practice is not hindered in any way.

Different monastic orders have different rules regarding the relationships between the monastics and their respective families. In the Fo Guang Shan order, candidates who wish to join the order are required to first seek the permission of their parents. Then, even after joining the order, monastics continue to visit with their families. When the mother of Venerable Tzu Jung was sick and dying, it was Tzu Jung, one of eleven children, who took care of her mother in her final months. Thus, while monastics may not express their love for their families in conventional ways, they do not love their families any less than laypeople.

When we love, we should avoid being limited to the narrow definition of love or trapped in the limitations of emotions. Love should never bind a person in shackles; it should always inspire freedom and not restrict it. The Buddha teaches us to love and yet remain free so that we may spread the emotional wealth we have for a few to all sentient beings.

(iv) To love one's parents to the best of one's abilities
The Buddha's disciple, Maudgalyayana, was a faithful and respectful son. After his mother passed away, he learned with his supernatural powers that his mother was suffering in hell. His love for his mother was so great that he did not hesitate to go to hell to help console his mother in her suffering. His dedication to his mother so moved the Buddha that the Buddha told him that the united efforts of the whole sangha could alleviate his mother's suffering, as well as the suffering of other people's kin. This is the beginning of Ullambana. In this way, not only was Maudgalyayana able to save his mother, but many others were also able to help their deceased relatives. This level of family dedication is a direct manifestation of remarkable love.

Chan Master Taoji of the North Qi dynasty was another example of a devoted son. When he traveled about spreading the Dharma, he carried his teaching materials as well as his mother in baskets suspended from a bamboo pole placed across his shoulders. When others offered him a hand, he would politely decline and say, "This is my mother who gave me life and raised me. I should be the one to take care of her." Chen Zunsu of the Tang Dynasty was a very accomplished Chan master as well as being a very loving and attentive son.

There are countless examples of selfless love for one's parents. The faithful and reverent love children have for their parents is a true and pure form of emotion. It is also a manifestation of what extraordinary love is.

(v) To love one's students as oneself

The following examples serve to show how past masters loved their students and followers. To teach and train their students, they used varying methods and seized every opportunity possible. In a relationship between a student and teacher, what may appear to some as methods that are mean and pointless are actually compassionate and intelligent strategies to empower students with wisdom and fortitude. If the same expectations and criticisms were handed down by a teacher with a cruel heart or malicious intentions, then certainly the methods employed would be unacceptable. However, with deep concern for the growth and cultivation of students, many teachers use what could be considered extreme tactics. In the presence of such love and dedication, the bond between teachers and students is forever sealed.

It is recorded in the *Analects* how heart-broken Confucius was when he learned of the death of his student, Yan Hui. He wailed and said repeatedly, "The heavens have let me down!" His tears fully captured his feelings for his students. He was saddened by the premature death of his student and grieved at the loss of someone with great potential. His love for his student was most compassionate and remarkable.

Milarepa gives us another example of heroic love. Milarepa traveled far and wide looking for a teacher. After extensive search and travels, Milarepa finally found Marpa to be his Dharma teacher. His teacher asked him, "You said you want to call me your teacher. Let me ask you what you have to offer me?"

Milarepa prostrated himself respectfully and said, "I am going to offer you all that I engage in my body, speech, and mind."

With this, Marpa agreed to accept him as his disciple. One day, Marpa told Milarepa, "You are a strong young man. I want you to build me a stone house so that I can store all my sutras. Once it is completed, I will teach you the Dharma."

Milarepa was most delighted. When he asked his teacher for a sketch of what he wanted, his teacher told him, "I want you to go to the tip of the east face of the mountain and build me a circular house. The roads are steep and treacherous, but your hard labor can help you work off your bad karma."

Milarepa worked day in and day out. When the house was about half finished, his teacher came up the mountain. He took off his half-moon-shaped cape, folded it a few times, and left it on the floor. He then turned toward Milarepa and said, "This does not look like a good spot. I want you to take the house apart and start over again on the west face of the mountain. I want you to build me a house that looks like this garment here."

Frustrated and speechless, Milarepa complied. When he was about half-way done, his teacher again came up the mountain and said, "The house still does not look right. I want you to take this apart and move all the materials to the north face of the mountain. There I want you to build me a triangular-shaped house to symbolize what a true cultivator I am."

Milarepa again followed his teacher's direction. Rain or shine, he worked non-stop, hoping to finish the house. It was about one-third completed when his teacher came up the mountain and asked him, "Who told you to build this house?"

Nervously, Milarepa replied, "You personally asked me to build you this house."

The teacher looked puzzled. Scratching his head, he said, "Oh! I can't really recall anything like this. Why would I ask you to build me a triangular-shaped house at this poor location? It looks like the type of altar used by cults. Do you want to do me harm? Take it apart! Take it apart! I want you to go to the south side and build me a square-shaped house. I want it to be nine stories tall, on top of which is one more floor for storage, for a total of ten stories. Once it is completed, I will teach you the Dharma!"

With these few words, all of Milarepa's efforts were washed down the drain. In this way, building and deconstructing, again and again, many months and years passed. Milarepa was mentally exhausted and physically fatigued. Some of his fellow students could not bear to see him suffer alone and offered to help him move tiles and bricks. When the teacher found out, he exploded and scolded Milarepa, "I asked you to build me a house. Did I say that you could ask others for help? Why are you so lazy?" His teacher not only yelled at him, he also gave him a few blows with a club. When he could no longer bear the pain, Milarepa let out a little squeal. Instead of comforting him, the teacher continued to reprimand him, "Why are you crying? When you first came and wanted to be my student, did you not say that you wanted to offer me all your actions, speech, and thoughts? I am just striking what is mine, and I am only yelling at what is mine. What is there for you to cry about?"

What Milarepa had to endure is beyond our imagination; he tacitly accepted an enormous amount of hardship. After a few years, Milarepa attained enlightenment and became an arhat, or Buddhist saint. On the night that he attained enlightenment, his teacher embraced him, crying, "When I first saw you, I realized you were one of those rare individuals with great potential. This is why I had to put you through the toughest tests, so that you would soon attain enlightenment. When I reprimanded you, hit you, and was downright unreasonable toward you, my heart ached with pain. But when I thought about what you were learning and the good it would do you in the future, I had to hide my pain and continue to challenge you." What looked unreasonable on the surface was in fact a teacher's love for his student. Especially by today's standards, treating a student in this manner may seem shocking and impermissible, but this was a commonly accepted student–teacher relationship during this time and was always implemented with the student's best interest in mind. Never was it an attempt to overpower or humiliate a person. It was a way to teach through symbolism and direct experience, grooming students for greatness.

When I entered monkhood many years ago as a young man, I was lucky enough to be educated in a similar fashion. On the day when we entered the hall to be ordained, all the precept masters were seated in a row. I remember one of the precept masters asking us sternly,

"Today, you are here to be ordained. Are you coming here today because you want to or because your teacher wants you to?"

Someone immediately answered, "It is my desire to come here today to be ordained."

When the precept master heard his reply, he took up his rattan stick[6] and began beating this student. Afterwards, he said, "How dare you come here without being asked by your teacher!"

It was another precept master's turn; he asked us the same question, "Are you here today because you want to be here or because you were asked to come?"

The other students saw what had happened earlier, so one of them got smart. He stood up and said carefully, "Please be patient with me; I am here today because my teacher asked me to come."

He thought he was very clever; but, his answer was still not satisfactory. The precept master gave him a beating and said, "If your teacher had not asked you to come, does that mean that you would not be here today?"

While this event was shocking and confusing at first, upon reflection we understood that the precept master did have a point. Did we have to be asked to the ordination? Did we not have the commitment to enter monkhood on our own?

Next, it was another precept master's turn. Like the two before him, he asked us the same question. With both experiences behind us, we thought we knew better. One of us said, "My teacher did tell me to come to be ordained, but I myself also want to come." He thought that such an answer could not go wrong. He could never have guessed that his answer would also bring him the same punishment as the two students before him had suffered. After the punishment, the precept master said, "Now you are simply trying to be clever."

Next, we were told to appear before another precept master. This time, the question was quite different. The precept master asked, "Have you ever violated the precept of killing?" Now, killing is a very serious offense, so we all shook our heads and said, "No, we have never violated the precept of killing."

The precept master then said, "Impossible! Are you telling me that you have never swatted a fly or stepped on an ant before? It is obvious that all of you are lying." With this, the precept master gave each of us a few strokes. I guessed he was right. We were not telling the whole truth, and we deserved to be punished. Then, another precept master asked us if we had violated the precept of killing. This time we replied, "Yes teacher, we have violated the precept of killing."

"This is a violation of the precepts and calls for punishment." With these words, the precept master gave each one of us a few strokes with a whip. As the day progressed, we did not want to answer any questions put before us. Helplessly, we just said, "Teacher, if you want to punish us, please do so."

Again, on the surface, this teaching method looks ridiculous and unreasonable. As it turned out, our teachers were intentionally unreasonable to teach us to let go of our reasoning intellect. They refused to cater to our feelings in order to teach us how to deal with our emotions. If we could surrender ourselves in the face of such drastic measures, then would we not learn to be more flexible and open-minded in all situations? Their demonstration of irrationality was, in fact, a tool to teach us to let go of our stubborn delusions. It was out of compassion that our teachers were so unfeeling. Looking back, I was indeed very lucky to have had the opportunity to be trained under the old school. The training was tough and painful, but without pain, how could there be greatness? The stringent test we had to go through was a blessing. When I look at the youth of today, I feel sorry for them. They do not have the opportunity to be so tested; the education of today does not instill in our youth the spirit of toughness and endurance. Discipline, when coupled with compassion and remarkable love, is a means for teachers to truly prepare their students for greatness in the future. The sacred relationship between a teacher and a student is a special kind of affinity; it may appear unbalanced, but it is one of the deepest and most treasured bonds.

The heroic love we have discussed here is just one level of love among many. When we extend our love from loving our immediate friends and relatives to loving our fellow community members, and then to all sentient beings, our love matures until it is infinite in breadth and depth. In this way, basic love first transforms into heroic love, which further matures into enlightened love, and here our natural and unbounded capacity to love without reserve is revealed. We can all love and be loved in this way; it is only a matter of discovering this truth.

3. *Enlightened Love*: A lot of us have heard about Ksitigarbha Bodhisattva. Before he became a bodhisattva, he cultivated himself in the hills of Jiuhua in Anhui. This was a region of very steep terrain and few people. At that time, there was a young boy living with him. One day, this

youngster could no longer bear to live in such isolation, so he asked to leave the temple and return to the village below. Ksitigarbha escorted the youngster down the mountain and offered him a poem as a parting gift. From the sentiments of the poem, we can see the transcendental love that bodhisattvas have for us. The poem goes like this:

> Within the quiet gates of this temple you long for
>   your family;
> As you descend the mountain, you say goodbye to
>   this temple in the clouds.
>
> You love to ride bamboo horses within bamboo
>   fences
> Rather than collect shimmering sand in this land
>   of gold.
>
> Do not try to pick up the moon in the water while
>   filling the vase;
> Or try to play with the flowers in the water while
>   washing the basin in the pond.
>
> Go, and do not shed a tear for me;
> This old man has the clouds in the sky to keep him
>   company.

In the first stanza, Ksitigarbha captures the feelings of the youngster: how lonely he is within the gates of the quiet temple and the heartfelt reasons why he wants to return to his home in the village. In the second stanza, with utmost empathy, Ksitigarbha cautions the youth as to what he is giving up by leaving the temple. He acknowledges the little boy's understandable desire to ride bamboo horses and play games rather than cultivate himself within the walls of a remote temple. In the third stanza, Ksitigarbha leaves words of advice for the youngster to keep in mind. He tells the little boy that when he takes a vase to the river to fill it up with water, he will see the reflection of the moon in the water. He warns the boy not to try to pick up the moon in the water, for it is just a reflection. He is implying that life in the world is illusory, too. Ksitigarbha also tells the boy that when he washes the basin in the pond, he should be careful not to mistake the reflections of trees and flowers in the water for a lush world in the pond. In the fourth stanza, Ksitigarbha comforts the youngster so that he will not feel guilty about leaving. He tells him to go and not to feel sorry for him.

Although Ksitigarbha lived in the quiet temple on the mountain, he could still find company in the fleeting fog and the floating clouds of the sky. Each word of the poem was superbly chosen and rich in meaning; each word was a lyrical manifestation of enlightened love.

From this example, we can see the love and affection bodhisattvas and arhats have for us. The feelings Ksitigarbha had for the little boy were multi-dimensional. He knew how the little boy felt, provided him with guidance, and even comforted him. He gave the boy his full support, without expecting anything in return. When bodhisattvas freely give their love and compassion, they never wonder what they will receive, nor do they hope for any reciprocity. Many people, unfortunately, do not yet know how to go beyond themselves and love without expectations. They only extend their love to others in the hope that they will then be given something. This kind of love is impure and infused with ulterior motives. It suppresses and oppresses people, rather than helping them toward complete freedom.

The kind of love that bodhisattvas give is something that we can not only aspire to imitate—in fact, we can imitate it! But, unlike bodhisattvas, whose enlightened love transcends all discriminations and dualities, we tend to focus our love on those we take a liking to, intentionally keeping a distance between ourselves and those we are not fond of. The concepts of rejection and discrimination no longer exist for bodhisattvas; they love everyone naturally and unconditionally. Still trapped in distinctions, we usually size up whether or not we have affinity for a person immediately upon meeting him or her. With someone that we have a good rapport with, we can spend hours in conversation. With those whom we don't have much in common with, even a short conversation is often punctuated by moments of "awkward silence," and good intentions are often misread. While it is easy to be kind and friendly to those we like, the Buddha teaches us to earlier "cultivate loving-kindness without conditions and ground compassion in oneness." True affinity is not picking and choosing whom we like and don't like; it is deeply connecting with all beings. When we do not limit our love to only our circle of family and friends, and instead embrace everyone, we are energizing affinity's great potential. We can model ourselves after the Buddha, who is always there to answer everyone's pleas, without discrimination. True compassion knows no discrimination, and in the bodhisattva spirit, we should be kind to friends and foes alike.

When Venerable Daoji of the Tang Dynasty was the abbot of the Fugan Temple in Yizhou, he opened the temple to many lepers, many of whom had open and infected sores. Venerable Daoji was not at all repelled by their condition; he even lived and ate with them. He also dressed their sores and helped them with their baths. Some of his disciples made excuses and tried to keep their distance from the lepers. Finally, someone asked the venerable, "Venerable, you spend time with the lepers every day. Are you not afraid that you will also become infected?"

Venerable Daoji smiled gently and said, "What we call clean or dirty is the result of our discriminating mind. If we do not have any dislikes in our minds, how can aversions arise? When our mind is pure, everything and everywhere is pure. If a monk like myself cannot even let go of this bit of delusion and let compassion arise in its place, I should be ashamed of myself for not living in accordance with the Dharma."

Such is the love of arhats and bodhisattvas. Their love and kindness are not limited only to their families and friends or to those who are labeled as lovable by the general population. Their lives touch many people they hardly know, and they love even those who are considered outcasts. Every breath they take is a breath of affinity; every move they make is a manifestation of love. Their acceptance is all-encompassing, their compassion knows no discrimination, and their view of self and others is rooted in equality. This is truly what we call compassion that is grounded in oneness.

I wish to share another interesting example with you. Mahakasyapa was one of the Buddha's great disciples. He was also an arhat. Mahakasyapa's parents, who were very affluent, wanted him to get married. Getting married was really not in Mahakasyapa's plans, for he wanted to dedicate his life to Buddhist cultivation. After being repeatedly pressured by his parents, he had no choice but to appease them. In order to delay the event, he asked a goldsmith to sculpt a statue of a beautiful young maiden. He took the sculpture to his parents and told them that he would marry only if he could find someone as elegant as the gold sculpture. In order to get their son to marry, his parents had no choice but to honor his request. They proceeded to ask a few servants to carry the sculpture around the country looking for someone that could match its beauty. The servants first spread word that the golden statue was really an image of a deva and would bring good luck to all young maidens who would come to pay their respects. This way, all young maidens would feel compelled to visit this wonderful statue, and, indeed, they eagerly came forward. Among the many who came, there was one who was so striking in her beauty that the gold statue paled in comparison. She was the beautiful maiden Bhadda Kapilani. The servants finally asked for the permission of her parents and brought her back to Mahakasyapa's parents.

Mahakasyapa had no choice but to keep his promise to his parents, and the two were married. As it turned out, this young lady also wanted to dedicate her life to cultivation, and she confessed her wish to Mahakasyapa. "This is really my parents' idea," she said. "They wanted me to marry you because of your family's wealth. As for me personally, I would rather live a life of spiritual cultivation." When Mahakasyapa heard this, he told her, "Good. I am very relieved. I also want to live a life of self-cultivation. Since this is what we both wish for, why don't we devote our lives to this practice." Thus, though they were husband and wife in name, they both continued their own course of self-cultivation.

After twenty years, when both sets of parents had passed away, Mahakasyapa and Bhadda Kapilani finally got their wish to renounce the household life and live a monastic life. They became a bhiksu and a bhiksuni respectively. Although Bhadda Kapilani became a bhiksuni, her beauty still attracted the attention of many men. When she went out to beg for alms, men would follow her and tease her. She was so taken aback by all the unwanted attention that she dared not go out to beg for alms. When Mahakasyapa saw what was happening to the woman whom he had called his wife once upon a time, he felt compassion for her and shared with her whatever food he received from his alms round. Others misread his compassion and began to circulate rumors by saying, "Look! They said they were only husband and wife in name, but they are still such a loving couple even though they are now in the sangha." Bhadda Kapilani lamented that her physical beauty was in fact a burden, so she disfigured herself in the hope that she could become a bhiksuni who was ugly in appearance but beautiful in cultivation. From this, we can see that the enlightened love and affection of arhats is different from the ordinary way we normally perceive love.

It is a common misconception to think that arhats, who are no longer bound by worldly emotions, are *without* emotions. This is not true at all. Like the Buddha, arhats have severed the ties of emotions, but they certainly still experience them. They are enlightened individuals who are rich in personality and true to their character. When we say arhats are empty of emotions, what we mean is that they have transcended the limited scope of conventional love and expanded their love for a few to a limitless and selfless compassion for all. When love is parochial, finite in capacity, and limited in scope, it does not do justice to human potential for unblemished and unlimited affinity with our fellow beings; it does not reflect the wondrous and boundless Dharma. From loving one's self, spouse, children and family, we should all extend our love to the Dharma and all sentient beings. True love is the touching of others' lives and the giving of ourselves for all.

4. *The Buddha's Kind of Love*: As a fully enlightened individual, what was the Buddha's emotional life like? What kind of love did he give? How far did his affinity reach? What was the capacity of his heart?

The Buddha loved everyone, friends and foes alike, equally and without discrimination. He gave this love without reservation, understanding that love and affinity are infinitely available. Before the Buddha renounced his household life, he was married to Princess Yasodhara of Devadaha. Many years after the Buddha left home and attained enlightenment, he went back to his hometown to see his family. Princess Yasodhara had not seen the Buddha for all these years and wondered how her husband had changed. Filled with hope and uncertainty, she was anxious about what to say to the Buddha, who had once been her husband. After the Buddha met with his father, the imperial court, and various royal cousins, he finally met with Princess Yasodhara. She thought to herself, "I really must express my true feelings and ask him why he left me." However, when Princess Yasodhara saw the majestic look of the Buddha, she immediately understood his pure intentions and could not help herself from kneeling down before him. The Buddha looked at her and said to her in a calm and stately tone of voice, "Yasodhara, I have to ask for your forgiveness for what I did to you. Though my leaving home to cultivate myself was not fair to you, I am most true to all sentient beings. Now, I ask you to rejoice for me, for it had been my wish for many kalpas to realize the truth of life and the universe and become the Buddha. My wish is to preach the Dharma and help all sentient beings, including yourself, cross the sea of suffering." His voice was compassionate, his appearance was resplendent, and the meaning of his words transcended ordinary love. Everyone was moved, and eventually Yasodhara also renounced her household life. From the way in which the Buddha handled his relationship with Yasodhara, we can see that to truly love a person is to help him or her grow and stay on the right path and introduce him or her to extraordinary love—love that is immeasurably beyond basic love.

You may already know that the Buddha's mother died seven days after giving birth to the Buddha. The Buddha, who had always wanted to preach the Dharma to his mother to thank her for delivering him into this world, finally fulfilled his wish and went to Trayastrimsas Heaven to preach the Dharma to her. When King Suddhodana, the father of the Buddha, passed away, all the princes expressed their desire to be pallbearers. Though the Buddha was the fully enlightened one and was most revered, he still insisted on being one of the pallbearers for his father. When people saw the Buddha serving as a pallbearer, everyone was very touched. The Buddha was indeed a devoted son and a respectable individual. Even as a fully enlightened individual, he never regarded himself as being too important or too spiritually cultivated to attend to his parents, even in small ways. He gave us a very good example of how to love and honor our parents.

The Buddha did not just love his family or those who were near and dear to him; he also loved those who were hostile toward him. His love for the people who caused him trouble was neither less than nor different from his love for those who were kind to him. When one understands that there is no maximum capacity for loving, one's friends and enemies are received with the same openness. Though the Buddha's cousin, Devadatta, treated him like an enemy, the Buddha did not bear any grudges against him. In fact, the Buddha used to tell everyone that Devadatta was his good teacher and was instrumental in helping him with his cultivation. Most of us are inclined to scorn and resent those who oppose us, instead of viewing their negativity as an opportunity to practice. Without darkness, how do we appreciate the illumination of light? Without evil, how do we appreciate the goodness of truth?

The Buddha did not just extend his compassion to the rich and the mighty; he was equally compassionate to all sentient beings without discrimination. When his students were sick, the Buddha would prepare the medication or deliver water to them. When older bhiksus failed in their eyesight and could not mend their clothes, the Buddha would personally help them thread needles and sew garments. The Buddha loved his disciples as a loving mother cares for her children. To his disciples, the Buddha was a source of light and strength. The Buddha is most compassionate and gives us limitless hope!

The Buddha was also a very patient teacher and adapted his teachings to the student and the occasion. When Nidhi, who made his living disposing of refuse for others, felt inadequate and tried to avoid the Buddha, the Buddha purposely went out of his way to meet up with him. With Ksullapanthaka, who was very slow and had trouble even memorizing a simple gatha, the Buddha spent extra time teaching the Dharma to him. When his disciple Mahakatyayana, who was preaching the Dharma in another area, sent one of his young students to pay respect to the Buddha, the Buddha made sure that this young student was well cared for. The Buddha told his disciples, "Now that the young student of Mahakatyayana has arrived, please set up a cot next to my bed for him to rest for the night." The great Buddha found time for everyone, even for a young student whom he just met. In showing his concern for the youngster, the Buddha was also showing his love for his disciple who was away teaching the Dharma. The Buddha always, without fail, showed enormous care and concern for others. The Buddha often thought about Aniruddha, who lost his sight because of long hours of cultivation and not getting enough rest. Only after Aniruddha attained supernatural vision did the Buddha stop worrying about him. The Buddha also worried about his cousin Ananda, who was very handsome and often attracted the unwanted attention of women. Only after Ananda became successful in his cultivation did the Buddha feel a sigh of relief for his cousin. Through all of these examples, we can see that the Buddha is a model of love for us to follow as we go through life, establishing new relationships and nurturing those that already exist, never excluding anyone from our limitless ability to love. The Buddha was a pro at living affinity, and we could all transform our lives and the lives of others by following in his footsteps.

Love and affection are infinitely valuable. I hope that you have now gained a more thorough understanding of the various levels of love and affection that we can aspire to. Some people describe how people love this way: Young people love with their words, middle-aged people love with their actions, and elderly people love with their hearts. This means that as we age, our love matures. Spiritual development also deepens and expands our love. Love starts at home. We love our spouse, our children, and our siblings. From here, we extend our love to our relatives and friends. Further, our love encompasses all human beings and then all beings. From a possessive kind of love, love matures into a giving kind of love, and finally into the enlightened love that bodhisattvas and Buddhas have for everyone. This kind of love is the great compassion that is described by the saying, "I will not seek pleasure just for myself. I long for all sentient beings to be free of suffering."

Love is like water. On the one hand, it can nurture our lives; on the other hand, it can drown us. Thus, if we do not know how to love properly, love can bring us many problems and ruin our lives. If we are ordinary and selective about whom we love, instead of embracing all beings, the vast dimensions of love are hardly actualized. How do we love properly? Let me offer the following four guidelines:

- *Love wisely*—We should use our wisdom to purify our love.

- *Love compassionately*—We should use our compassion to manifest our love.
- *Love in accordance with the Dharma*—We should use the Dharma to guide our love.
- *Love morally*—We should use morals and ethics to direct our love.

Love is such an important subject of our lives. How do we love selflessly and offer our love to all? How do we transform a possessive love into a giving love, to a love for the Dharma? How do we purify our love from one of discrimination to one of great compassion? How do we love in the spirit of this common saying: "Cultivate loving-kindness without conditions, and ground compassion in oneness"? How do we manifest the true potential of affinity? These are very important questions for us to ponder! When we seek to go beyond ourselves and offer our love and affection in service to the community, then our lives and the lives of others will be more rewarding and more joyful!

❧ CHAPTER THREE ❧

Living Affinity through Protecting the Environment

W E HAVE DISCUSSED THE fact that relationships create the atmosphere in which we live, and, therefore, how we conduct ourselves and treat others determines the quality of our lives and the lives of others. As we move from ordinary love to extraordinary love, and from perceived distance to true affinity, the atmosphere of our community turns into something harmonious, joyous, and ultimately affirming. This is true not only of the figurative atmosphere, but also of the literal, or physical, atmosphere: our environment. In other words, the harmony and beauty of the environment also depend on the skillful development of relationship—our relationship to the earth. As a foundational principle, it is important to realize that affinity is not only possible with people; affinity is a deep and profound relationship *with all phenomena*—including our precious earth. Therefore, Buddhism not only advocates loving and building affinity with our fellow human beings, but teaches us to love and live in harmony with our environment, too. When we say, "We are all one, and we exist in dependence," we are not merely talking about human beings. The sutras say, "All living beings have Buddha-nature," and, "All beings, sentient or not, have the same perfect wisdom." All existence is intimately intertwined; the survival of humans, animals, plant life, and our very earth depends upon mutual affinity. Every action we undertake, every thought we have impacts ourselves, others, and the earth.

This section on protecting the environment will offer many suggestions—some general, some specific—on how we can live on this earth with minimum impact and maximum respect and, as a result, make natural affinity with all life the very essence of our existence. We will also explore how the purity of the mind and heart relate to the purity of the world. Our internal environment and our external environment are interconnected, and cannot arise independently. Most of the progress we have made in environmental protection is focused externally, but the important work actually lies within one's heart and spirit. Only when we have a healthy spiritual environment within can we be effective in protecting the physical environment. We need to develop internal affinity in order to be truly successful in environmental affinity. How can Buddhism help us to cultivate these relationships?

The Buddhist tradition of protecting the environment
Most people regard the Buddhist religion as conservative and passive. Many think that Buddhism only teaches

people to meditate, recite mantras, and be vegetarians. They do not associate the religion with active and progressive ideas such as environmental protection. In truth, Buddhism is a religion that embodies the spirit of environmental protection, and it has a long history of being active in such matters, reaching back to well before the concept became popular as a modern social cause.

Throughout its history, Buddhism has had a profoundly positive impact on the environment. In the Buddha's former life as a deer king, he laid down his own life to save that of a doe. A human king witnessed his compassion and was so moved that he designated the area as a wildlife sanctuary where hunting was forbidden. The Buddha also ceaselessly reminded his disciples to protect trees and animals. Over time, Buddhist temples and monasteries have followed the Buddha's teachings and the Buddha's example by caring for the great earth in various ways. Monastics have planted trees, dredged rivers, repaired roads, mended bridges and thoughtfully used and cared for natural resources. During discourses, monastics encouraged devotees to free captured animals, promoted vegetarianism, and reminded everyone to value the gifts of nature. There is a story about a bodhisattva who loved the environment so much that he feared polluting the great earth every time he discarded a piece of paper, feared disturbing the planet every time he uttered a phrase, and feared injuring the ground every time he took a step. His keen awareness of the environment provides a good role model for us.

From these actions, we see that monastics were environmental activists before the term "environmental protection" was coined. Their actions not only beautified the environment, but were also a form of practice. This tradition of nurturing the natural world and cultivating a deeper spiritual practice through performing environmentally kind deeds continues to this day. When we do our part to protect the environment, we invite beauty into the present moment and give future generations a fair chance to live peacefully and work happily on a healthy and thriving planet.

Protecting the environment does not always mean leaving it untouched, reserving it for viewing from a distance. We live on this planet and have to utilize the natural resources it offers. This, however, must be accomplished with utmost respect for nature. Venerable Mingyuan of ancient China planted thousands of trees along the Sizhou River[7] to prevent flooding. Venerable Daoyu of Luoyang saw that many ships had capsized along the Longmen Gorge on the Yellow River. To prevent further tragedy, he and his friend Bai Juyi rallied the local residents to widen the river in order to slow its flow. These two examples are well documented, but there were many similar environmental works that escaped recognition. In their travels, many monastics had forged paths through the jungle and laid steps over jagged mountains to ease the passage for future travelers. Without any fanfare, they worked to balance the needs of the environment with those of mankind, nurturing a harmonious relationship between human beings and the earth we live upon, and practicing the bodhisattva spirit of providing ease and convenience for all.

On March 4, 1992, during our annual Buddha's Light Conference, we held a workshop to promote "environmental and spiritual" protection. We encouraged everyone to start with beautifying one's mind and spirit and then extend outward to beautifying their environment. We offered twelve guidelines, as follows:

* *Speak quietly*—do not disturb others.
* *Keep the ground clean*—do not litter.
* *Keep the air clean*—do not smoke or pollute.
* *Respect oneself and others*—do not commit violent acts.
* *Be polite*—do not intrude upon others.
* *Smile*—do not face others with an angry expression.
* *Speak kindly*—do not utter abusive words.
* *Follow the rules*—do not seek exemptions or privileges.
* *Be mindful of your actions*—do not act unethically.
* *Consume consciously*—do not waste.
* *Be grounded*—do not live aimlessly.
* *Practice kindness*—do not create malice.

Furthermore, the International Buddha's Light Association, together with various governmental agencies in Taiwan, worked to preserve the local water source by campaigning for planting new trees and preserving existing ones. By planting new trees—two million to be exact—we were able to directly protect the water source. By recycling paper, we reduced the need to cut down trees, which also protected the water source.

When we Buddhists think of a pure, clean environment, we would naturally think of Amitabha's Western Pure Land. We can learn a lot about environmental protection from Amitabha Buddha. On his path as a bodhisattva, Amitabha made forty-eight great vows. Through the strength of these vows, he manifested the Western Pure Land, a land of unparalleled beauty and peace. The ground is covered with radiant gold, pagodas are built with precious gems, and all facilities are in excellent condition. In Western Pure Land there is only public good and no public harm. There is only beauty: no toxins, noise, or pollution. The weather is cool and pleasant, and the water has eight wonderful qualities: clear, cool, sweet, soft, soothing, peaceful, cleansing, and nourishing. The land is pure and the atmosphere is serene. Everyone in the Pure Land is kind, is in full health of mind and body, has ageless longevity, and is free of the three poisons. No one would ever consider chopping down trees, and the landscape reflects such thoughtfulness. This pure land is a place that many of us aspire to, and, in fact, with mindful and compassionate living, we can create a pure land right here on earth. Clearly, we say that Amitabha Buddha is a wise teacher in maintaining a sound mind and a healthy environment.

Inner sanctity and outer ecological balance
As we strive to cultivate a positive relationship with the environment, we should first realize there are two facets to the journey—preserving inner sanctity and maintaining outer ecological balance. While there are various ways to achieve both of these things, we must realize that they are not mutually exclusive; the internal environment influences the external environment, and the external environment affects the internal one. We have all had the experience of becoming more calm and happy when we are in an area of pristine, natural beauty, untouched by any sort of desecration. And, with a pure and peaceful inner life, the kind that seeks to generate affinity with all things, one is naturally compelled to care for the external world.

We alone are responsible for our inner peace. To do this, we have to practice internal environmental protection and see into the emptiness of the three poisons—greed, anger, and ignorance. External environmental protection, such as natural habitat preservation, air purification, water source cleanup, noise pollution control, trash management, and protection from radiation must rely upon the joint efforts of everyone. If all people united in a common focus to honor the environment instead of taking advantage of its bounty—which is swiftly disappearing—our earth would be rapidly transformed and return to the environmental paradise it once was.

We will first discuss maintaining outer ecological balance. There are two main ways to protect the environment: treasure life and conserve resources. One of the Five Precepts is to refrain from killing, or in other words, to treasure life. In the *Brahma Net Sutra*, it states, "When a follower of the Buddha exercises compassion and sets a life free, he should recite, 'All males are my fathers. All females are my mothers. Rebirth after rebirth, they give me life. All beings in the six realms of existence are my parents. Killing animals for meat is the same as killing my parents, indirectly killing the source of my body.' If you witness someone killing an animal, you should save the animal, relieve its suffering, and spread the work of the Buddha and the bodhisattvas to save all beings." The precept to refrain from killing is the expression of respect for all sentient life. At its most basic level, the practice as stated is not to kill. To take this a step further, we should actively save life and help those in need. When we see a hurt animal, we should care for it so that it may feel safe and strong again. We need to have a proactive, compassionate, and protective attitude toward animals. Nowadays, people have exotic tastes and would not hesitate to eat anything that moves, regardless of whether it is a creature of the sky, land, or water. This type of indiscriminate slaughter and consumption not only defiles the inner spirit, but also disturbs the outer balance in our natural environment and increases the violent energy in the world. Therefore, to raise the quality of life we should promote respect for and protection of all living beings and increase the energy of affinity in the world.

Buddhist masters of the past were in tune with human beings' inherent connection with all forms of life in the six realms of existence, especially animals. They were at ease in the company of lions and tigers. Master Huiyue of the Sui Dynasty frequently spoke to wild animals about the Dharma. Tigers became tame and lay down like kittens at his feet. Master Cizang lived alone in the mountains and always made it a point to save animals who were hurt. When he ran out of food, birds would bring him fruit. In the *Connected Discourses of the Buddha*, there is a story of a novice monk who was near the end of his life span. One day, he saw a group of ants drowning in water and reached out to save them. Through his act of compassion, he gained a long life. All these stories serve as reminders for us to act with compassion. Treasuring life is a basic moral principle of being human and is the best tool for transforming anger, violence, and sadness into tranquility.

In addition to nurturing and protecting animal life, we should also treasure plant life. Even a blade of grass is vital because it purifies the air we breathe. We must not neglect any life, because each contributes to the delicate balance of which we are all a part. When one strand in the web is adversely affected, the whole web experiences the negative impact. Conversely, when one piece of the web is positively affected, the entire web benefits. When we save a tree, we make the world a little bit greener, provide a home for countless creatures, and create more fresh air to breathe and enjoy. Protecting life also means that we should be gentle to insentient objects, such as mountains and rivers and even everyday household items. A table, chair, or towel should be treated conscientiously, because if we do not take proper care of these items and they last only five years instead of the intended ten, we are indirectly wasting and harming "life." If you've never considered developing affinity with a dishtowel, perhaps now is the time to start. A harmonious relationship with the environment requires a harmonious relationship with each and every creature and object that exists within it.

In addition to treasuring life, we can protect the environment by conserving resources. In our daily life, it is so easy to be wasteful. Consider paper as an example. A tree that takes ten years to grow can be chopped down in a matter of hours. For every ton of paper recycled, we save twenty trees. We can also save trees by using both sides of a sheet of paper. Trees are very important to our environment. They provide us with shade, play a key role in the water cycle, and enable us to breathe—a very important thing indeed!

Conservation yields benefits not only to the environment, but also to us directly. How much we have in life depends on our past actions, or karma. Karma can be compared to a bank account. You have to first make deposits and accumulate some savings before you can make a withdrawal. Conservation creates tangible savings in our karma accounts. In this regard, I can speak from personal experience. Many devotees have complimented me on my intelligence. I believe my intelligence is a result of my past conservation efforts. When I was still a young novice monk, I was very frugal with my writing paper. On one piece of paper, I would not only write on both sides but also between the lines. Sometimes I would even use a different colored pen to write over existing text so I wouldn't waste the paper. It was only when I could no longer decipher my own writing that I regretfully threw away a piece of paper. I believe the good karma that I accrued by making the most of each piece of paper brought me the gift of intelligence. Therefore, everyone can begin saving in his or her "karma account" by taking care of the gifts that nature has given us.

To reduce the consumption of natural resources, there are many things we can do with minimal effort. For example, instead of using disposable paper plates and plastic utensils, we can use reusable ones. Styrofoam and plastic are not environmentally friendly. They are not biodegradable, sitting for centuries in landfills and producing carcinogenic gases if incinerated. We should all contribute to our planet's health by using fewer disposable items.

Another way to conserve resources is to recycle. We can recycle paper, aluminum cans, plastic bottles, glass jars, and much more as recycling technology becomes more sophisticated and creative. As more people recycle, awareness will be heightened, generating momentum for the cause. By practicing recycling, we practice the teachings of the Buddha, demonstrate our love and concern for the environment, strengthen the connection between people, and help spread environmental awareness.

In terms of specific actions that we all can do, I want to offer the following suggestions for building affinity with the environment:

Consume moderately and do not purchase more than you can use: always be grateful for that which nourishes you.

Maintain your car and follow emission guidelines: faithfully maintain the purity of the air.

Minimize the use of disposable items and reduce the amount of trash you produce: consciously decrease the need for landfills.

Take shorter showers: conserve the earth's water supply.

Do not litter: respect the pristine appearance of the land.

Use energy-saving light bulbs or fixtures: enjoy the glow of candles whenever possible.

Reduce usage of your home air conditioner: be at ease in any temperature.

Use your car's air conditioner as little as possible: automobile air conditioning systems are one of the main emitters of chlorofluorocarbons into the earth's ozone layer—delight in the refreshing air from an open window.

Recycle as much as possible and use more recycled materials: decrease the need for relying upon new resources.

Choose durable and fuel-efficient tires: maximize the life span of all resources.

Bring your own shopping bags when shopping: make the most use out of a product.

There are countless ways to be mindful as we tread upon this precious earth. When we put forth a conscious effort to conserve resources, we help to maintain what is still pristine in our environment and reverse the damage already done.

In addition to protecting the physical environment, we have to take good care of our internal spiritual environment. When one suffers, the other suffers; when one is at ease, the other is at ease. The *Vimalakirti Sutra* says, "If one wants to be in a pure land, one should purify the mind. When the mind is pure, the land is pure." This means that the environment we live in is a reflection of our state of mind. To be successful in the movement to better the environment, we must not neglect to tend to our inner spirit. From time without beginning, greed, hatred, jealousy, and malice have enshrouded our pure nature. We must work to turn greed into generosity, hatred into compassion, jealousy into tolerance, and malice into respect. When we change the way we think and the way we see the world, what we see, hear, and touch will take on a different quality. Our true nature knows nothing but affinity; our true nature is affinity itself. Our life's work is to realize this inherent, boundless capacity.

We should care for our body and mind as we care for the physical environment. After all, our body can be compared to the great earth. The circulatory system is like a river, flowing ceaselessly to transport nutrients to various parts of the body. The lungs are like forests in reverse. They take in oxygen and breathe out carbon dioxide. Bones are like mountains, giving protection to our many delicate organs. Cells are like little forest animals, moving about with vitality. Our body is like a village with the six inhabitants of eyes, ears, nose, tongue, skin, and mind. The mind is like a village chief, directing and influencing the other inhabitants. If we want good physical health and utmost environmental health, we should start with our mental health. When we have inner stability, then our body and the earth will know peace.

How do we maintain purity in our internal environment? We simply have to be mindful of the Buddha. If you have the Buddha in your heart, everything you see in the world is the sight of the Buddha, everything you hear is the sound of the Buddha, everything you say is the word of the Buddha, and everything you do holds the compassion of the Buddha. Although we live in a world full of negativity, if we know how to preserve our inner sanctity, we can be more like the Buddha. Like a pristine lotus that rises out of the mud of a pond, we can rise above the distractions of the world. We will no longer struggle to develop affinity with others and with the world; true affinity will be our natural and everlasting way of being.

We have discussed many aspects of environmental protection and affinity. I would like to conclude with the following lines:

> *Value every word*—they are the roots of dignity.
> *Treasure every grain of rice*—this is the way of wealth.
> *Speak with care*—it is the basis of happiness.

Protect even the smallest form of life—this is the cause of longevity.

❧ CHAPTER FOUR ❧

Living Affinity with the Material Aspect of Life

WHILE IT MAY SEEM preposterous to develop affinity with our dishtowels, our relationship to the material world is hardly an insignificant aspect of building positive relationships *with all phenomena.* Just as we are not separate from the interconnected web of human relationships, and just as we cannot live apart from our environment, so are we connected to our material world. The clothing we wear, the food we eat, the accommodations we live in, the transportation we rely on, the finances we deal with, and so forth are all a part of our existence. Our relationship to these things can be positive or negative, harmonious or discordant, harmful or beneficial, ignorant or mindful. When we are living with affinity, one dollar is a blessing; when we have no affinity, even a million dollars isn't enough. An affinity with the material aspect of life will help us to maintain a healthy balance and a helpful attitude about possessions and money. Are we content with our material possessions, or do we always crave more? Are we grateful for what we have, or do we take it for granted? Are we able to distinguish between our needs and our wants? Are we using our wealth for the benefit of others, or for our own personal desires? These are important questions to consider as we examine our relationship to the material world and learn how to build affinity, even with our dishtowels.

To begin with, we will look to the Buddha's relationship with the material world. Even the Buddha, the fully enlightened one, participated in the material world and therefore had basic needs to be met—namely clothing, food, shelter, and the means to get from place to place. While we share the same needs as the Buddha, these needs took on a different meaning in the case of the Buddha. As we will learn below, the Buddha's relationship to the material world was a practice in itself. Through understanding the Buddha's mindful and appreciative relationship to the basic necessities of life, we can begin to learn a new way to live in affinity with the material world.

The material side of living according to the *Diamond Sutra*

The *Diamond Sutra* says, "At mealtime, the Blessed One put on his robe, took the alms bowl, and entered the city of Sravasti. Having begged for alms in due order, he returned to his place. After his meal, he put away his robe and alms bowl, washed his feet, and sat in a cross-legged posture...." This opening of the *Diamond Sutra* describes a typical day of the Buddha. On the surface, there is nothing unusual about his daily routine. If we look deeper, however, we will see that the way the Buddha carried out these activities is actually a skillful means to teach us how to conduct our daily lives and expand our capacity to interact with the material world in a transcendental way, instead of our habitual and ordinary way.

Putting on the robe and taking up the alms bowl signifies the observance of precepts. Entering the city of Sravasti to beg for alms is an illustration of generosity—both on the part of those who gave alms and on the part of the Buddha teaching them the Dharma. To beg for alms in due order exemplifies patience, for the Buddha begged for alms in an orderly fashion, from house to house and not according to personal preference. Regardless of the condition of the food received, the Buddha consumed the food with thankfulness. This is patience, too. Taking his meal, putting away his robe and alms bowl, and washing his feet reflects the perfection of diligence. Sitting in a cross-legged position corresponds to the perfection of meditative concentration. Through his daily activities, the Buddha showed us that the Dharma is present in each of the four basic necessities of life. In this way, the Buddha integrated the six perfections in his daily life and built affinity with the material world.

During the Tang Dynasty, there was a Chan master named Zhaozhou. Once when someone asked him to explain the Dharma, Zhaozhou replied, "Go and eat." On another occasion of being asked to explain the Dharma, he said, "Go and wash dishes." When a third person asked the Chan master to show him the wondrous teachings of Chan, Zhaozhou told him, "Go and sweep the floor." Eating, washing dishes, or sweeping the floor are trivial daily activities that we all have experienced. So, where is the Dharma? The Dharma is in our everyday life. Most people do not understand that their whole life—every action, every thought, every intention—can be a relationship with the Dharma. They neglect the way they conduct their daily lives and the Dharma that surrounds them; instead, they purposefully travel afar to seek the truth. During the course of Chan history, there were many masters who became enlightened while eating, cleaning up, or tilling the soil. There are yet other Chan masters who became enlightened while listening to the wind blowing against bamboo or the cries of a nearby child. In our pursuit of truth, while it is important that we study the sutras and learn from virtuous teachers, it is equally important that we do not ignore our everyday life. If we are mindful in our daily activities of putting on our clothes, eating, sleeping, and getting from place to place, we will come to realize that the Dharma is everywhere. In this way, we will know great ease and happiness in our relationship with the material world.

How do we see the Dharma everywhere and build affinity with the four basic necessities of life? First, let's talk about clothing. Most people put a lot of emphasis on the way they look. Just go to any department store, and you will be dazzled by the vast variety of clothing for sale. Clothes come in different colors, materials, and styles. Regardless of how much we spend on our wardrobe, it only makes us look good on the outside and does not change the inside whatsoever. Expensive clothing cannot mask one's internal delusions. One who is compassionate commands respect regardless of how he or she is dressed. Buddhism places emphasis on inner cultivation and teaches us to adorn ourselves with grace and elegance. Our internal beauty is like a wild orchid that emanates a fragrance for miles.

As far as food is concerned, the Buddha points out that our physical body is only the coming together of the four great elements and is without independent nature. While our physical body is empty in nature, we do need to take care of it, for without it we will not be able to practice. Once we understand that our body is empty in nature, we will consume food for the purpose of keeping our body healthy and not for indulging our senses. For this reason, the Buddha instructed his disciples not to spend time in preparing meals; instead, they should get the food they need for the day through their alms rounds. For modern lay practitioners, a simple diet that is consumed with sincere mindfulness and that does not harm other sentient beings is encouraged.

Venerable Hongyi of the Vinaya School had an excellent attitude in the way he looked at food. He never complained about anything and led a life of equanimity. One day, a Mr. Xia Mianzun,[8] a well-known educator of that time, saw the venerable eating his dinner. His dinner was most simple and consisted of a single dish of pickled vegetables. He felt sorry for the venerable and asked, "Don't you think that these pickled vegetables are a bit too salty?" To this, the venerable replied, "A salty taste has its own appeal." After dinner, the venerable poured himself a glass of water to drink. With his eyebrows knit, Mr. Xia asked, "Why not drink a cup of tea? Plain water is so bland." The venerable smiled and replied, "Yes, plain water is bland, but its blandness has its own special taste, too." The venerable lived a simple life of little want and great contentment. The way he viewed his food revealed not only that he had truly integrated the Dharma into his daily life, but also how joyous a life full of Chan can be. Most of us look at a life of subsistence as a burden, but Hongyi truly enjoyed what he had; he remains an excellent example of living affinity with the material world.

Now, let's examine what our view should be regarding accommodation. Some people live in palatial estates, while others crowd in small apartments. There is an old Chinese saying regarding our true needs, "A full meal during the day; a bed to sleep in for the night." If we discern the difference between what we need and what we want, we will see that our basic requirements are quite minimal. Regardless of whether we live in a penthouse or a small apartment, all that we need for the night is a mere three-by-six-foot space. According to a story related in Chapter 9 of Book VI of Confucius's *Analects*, one of Confucius's students, Yen Hui, was said to have lived a life consisting of "a bowl of rice, a gourdful of drink, and an abode on a humble lane. Many could not tolerate such bare subsistence, yet Hui would not change his life of joy a bit."

The founding father of the Ming Dynasty, Zhu Yuanzhang, once spent a period as a novice monk before he became emperor. One night, when he returned late to the temple, its doors were locked. He had no choice but to sleep on the ground outside the temple. While lying down, he looked up at the starry sky and had an inspiration, which he captured in this poem:

Sky as canopy, earth as blanket.
Sun, moon, stars accompany me to sleep.
Nighttime, dare not stretch my legs;
Fearing a misstep, shattering sky at bottom of sea.

Whether we live in a big house or a small house is not important. What matters is how big our hearts are. Someone who is selfish and discontented will always find fault with his or her circumstances, even if he or she lives in a nice, grand house. If we apply the Buddha's teachings to our daily life, then, regardless of how we live, where we are, and what we are doing, we will still find happiness within ourselves. The Venerable Cihang once wrote, "When one finds peace within oneself, north, east, south, and west are all good." With such a mindset, we feel at home wherever we are. One of the Buddha's disciples, Mahakasyapa, practiced a life of poverty and often spent his nights by tombstones without any sense of dissatisfaction or complaint.

Our mind also influences how we look at the various modes of transportation. Before the advent of the automobile, people used to marvel at the speed of a bicycle compared to that of walking. Now that the automobile is commonplace, we look at bicycles and think how slow they are. On the other hand, traveling by car does not come close to the speed we can achieve with air travel. Even in the case of air travel, we notice its speed mainly at takeoff and landing. Once we reach a steady cruising speed, we are hardly aware of how fast we are traveling. Our mindset plays a significant role in determining what we perceive as fast or slow. It seems that whenever we have to rush somewhere, we inevitably hit all the red lights. So, what is the fastest mode of transportation? Believe it or not, it is our heart and mind. The *Amitabha Sutra* says, "To the west, a hundred thousand million Buddha Lands away, there is a world called Ultimate Bliss." How can we possibly travel to a place as far away as a hundred thousand million

Buddha Lands? To this question, the *Amitabha Sutra* answers, "In an instant of pristine meditative concentration, one can be reborn in the World of Ultimate Bliss." From this, we see that the wondrous workings of our heart and mind are beyond our comprehension.

The Dharma teaches us that what we need and what we want are two very different things. When we are in charge of our mind, we will not let our indulgence in clothing, food, shelter, and transportation run circles around us. How we develop and manage our relationship to the material world is a practice in itself and can indeed help us to see the Dharma everywhere and in everything. We are on our way to building a positive relationship with all aspects of our lives and entering into the inherent affinity that exists between all beings and all phenomena. When we apply the Buddha's teachings to all aspects of daily life, we'll find happiness within ourselves and discover our natural and unlimited capacity for connection.

The material side of living according to the *Amitabha Sutra*

There is a common misperception that leading a spiritual life and applying the teachings means living meagerly and purposely cutting oneself off from any material comfort. To most people, Buddhism is a religion that only talks about emptiness and spiritual living and ignores the reality of existence in what we might call normal society. Some even close their minds to the religion because they are afraid that if they become Buddhists, they will have to give up their nice clothes and comfortable homes. They figure that if they have to give up all comforts to become a Buddhist, they should not bother. Actually, Buddhist practice takes on various forms, and undue emphasis on abstaining from possessing material goods without understanding the deeper significance of this practice will only serve to drive people away. In fact, if we read the *Amitabha Sutra*, we will see that Buddhism and material comfort that is acquired and utilized with the proper attitude are not mutually exclusive.

The *Amitabha Sutra* is a well-known sutra of the Pure Land School of Buddhism, and in it there are detailed descriptions of Amitabha's Pure Land of Ultimate Bliss. As mentioned earlier, the Pure Land is a place of grandeur, radiant with gold and jewels. The elevated standard of living in this Pure Land is beyond our imagination. From this sutra and the qualities of the Pure Land described therein, we learn that Buddhism is not just about suffering. In fact, the Pure Land School of Buddhism points out how we can be reborn into this World of Ultimate Bliss, a place of unparalleled happiness and unlimited splendor.

As far as suffering is concerned, there is no question that Buddhism speaks of suffering; this is merely stating the facts of life. Buddhism also goes a step further and teaches us how suffering can be a form of practice. It does not, however, equate suffering with practice, or state that we all have to go through pain to achieve liberation, or dictate that in order to be a truly cultivated individual one must live in poverty.

In regard to how we should manage our material wants and needs, Buddhism does not suggest that we have to unduly deprive ourselves. While a life of extreme self-mortification is spiritless and dull, Buddhism also stresses that we should not be self-indulgent in our material wants and needs. Desires can easily become insatiable. Once we have a comfortable house, we also want to drive a fancy car; now that we all have television sets, we long for central air-conditioning. From one desire to another, we can become enslaved to the material world, at the expense of our spiritual development. Thus, Buddhism does not endorse either a life of self-mortification or one of self-indulgence. While the *Amitabha Sutra* speaks of inconceivable comfort in the Pure Land, the environment is purely a means for furthering the practice of the Dharma and attaining Buddhahood; it is by no means an invitation to complacency and gluttony. When the *Diamond Sutra* says, "Let intentions arise without any clingings," it tells us that we need not give up everything; instead, it stresses the practice of the Middle Way. The Buddha teaches us to avoid the extremes of self-mortification as well as those of self-indulgence.

Acquiring, using, and measuring wealth

With a basic understanding that wealth is necessarily a deadly poison that we all should shun, let's explore how to have an ethical and beneficial relationship with wealth. Buddhism teaches us that money should be pursued in an ethical manner and always be used to better mankind. Within these parameters, the pursuit of affluence is not inconsistent with the Buddha's teachings.

In American vernacular, there is a saying that playfully captures the powerful influence that money has on people: "People mumble; money talks." Unfortunately, for some of us the temptation of money and the ways in which we use it may cause us to compromise our integrity and damage our precious relationships. Money problems have caused many rifts in relationships that were once cooperative and loving. We often read about family feuds that develop due to conflict over the distribution of an inheritance. If ethics are abandoned as we manage and relate to our finances, we are laying the foundation for great suffering and moral bankruptcy, even if our actual bank accounts are overflowing. How do we manage our finances prudently and ensure that our ethics are intact? I want to offer a Buddhist perspective on three areas of thought regarding wealth that can help us avoid an unhealthy relationship with money and instead develop one that engenders both spiritual development and deep affinity with others. At the same time, we will learn how to build a foundation for good fortune.

Acquiring wealth
While most of us wish for a comfortable life, not all of us will come into riches. Due to the Law of Cause and Effect, only those who have planted the karmic seeds of wealth are blessed with wealth. Cause always begets effect. How much wealth we have depends on a combination of how hard we work and our past karma. Wealth is not something that is bestowed by the gods. It is the fruit of past generosity. While almsgiving is the seed of wealth, hard work is the condition that nurtures the seed to fruition. We cannot change the past, but we can definitely change the future by our present actions. Even if one were to be handed millions of dollars, one would not be able to enjoy the riches unless the karmic seeds of wealth had been sown. The following is a Chinese folktale that serves to illustrate this point.

Once, there was a beggar who bought himself a lottery ticket. It turned out his ticket had the winning numbers.

When he found out that his ticket was the winning ticket, he was happy beyond words. In those days, there was a waiting period of half a month before the prize could be claimed. Since he lived on the street and had nowhere to safeguard his ticket, he hid it in his "begging stick."[9] During the next few days, he could not stop dreaming about what he would buy with the prize money. A car? A house? Expensive furniture? He wanted them all. One day, as he dreamed of how he would now be able to get married, settle down, and maybe even take his family abroad to travel, he found he had walked to the end of an ocean pier. As he stood on the pier watching the waves at sea, he could hardly wait any longer to claim his prize money. He looked at his stick and was disgusted with what it symbolized. He took the stick, held it over his head, and used all his might to throw it out to the sea. As he watched the waves carrying the stick out to sea, he let out all his pent-up anger about being poor by screaming, "From now on, I am going to be a rich man. I won't need you anymore!" Only when it was finally time to claim his prize did he remember that he had hidden his ticket in the stick that he had thrown into the sea. The beggar went crazy. His dream of becoming a rich man was so close, yet so far away.

How do we plant the karmic seeds of wealth? Let me tell you a story from the sutras. Mahakatyayana, noted for his talents in debate and persuasion, was one of the disciples of the Buddha. One day, while he was out on his alms round, he saw a poor old lady. He went up to her and asked, "I am here for alms, can you please be so kind as to give me some food?"

The old lady knitted her brow and replied, "I don't even have enough to eat; what can I give you?"

"You said you were poor. Why don't you give me your poverty?"

The old lady could not believe her ears. She asked, "What? How can I give you my poverty? Who would want it?"

"Give it to me. I want it," Mahakatyayana answered.

"How, then, do I give it to you?"

Mahakatyayana explained, "You give alms. When you give alms, you are planting the karmic seeds of wealth."

We cannot simply wish for wealth. The Buddha teaches that if we wish for wealth, we should plant the karmic seeds of wealth by giving alms. Previously, we discussed how giving alms is not just about the giving of money or material goods. When we give our time, our love, or our compassion, we are also giving alms. Thus, we all have the ability and means to plant the karmic seeds of wealth.

In addition to planting the karmic seeds of wealth by giving alms, the Buddha also teaches us to pursue wealth in an ethical manner. The Agamas speak of an incident that illustrates that wealth acquired unethically is as poisonous as a venomous snake. One day, when the Buddha and Ananda were out on their alms round, they came across a piece of gold on the road. Pointing to the gold piece, the Buddha said, "Ananda, look. There is a venomous snake over there." Looking in the direction of the gold, Ananda replied, "Yes, Lord Buddha, I see. That indeed is a snake." The Buddha nodded, and the two then continued on their alms round.

It so happened that a father and his son were working in a nearby field. When they overheard the Buddha's conversation with Ananda, they were curious and decided to see the snake for themselves. When they got to where the Buddha and Ananda had been standing earlier, they were pleasantly surprised to see, not a snake, but a gold piece. The father was ecstatic and said to his son, "This is no snake. The Buddha must have been mistaken. This is a piece of gold." He then picked up the gold and took it home with him.

It turns out that this piece of gold actually belonged to the king. A thief had broken into the treasury earlier and dropped the gold piece on the road as he made his escape. When the king found the missing gold in the farmer's possession, he arrested the farmer, assuming that he was the thief who had stolen it. It was then that the farmer finally understood that when wealth is not pursued in an ethical manner, it is like a poisonous snake—dangerous and deadly.

In the Noble Eightfold Path, the Buddha teaches us about right livelihood. The Buddha teaches that we should earn our living with integrity and ethics. We should not engage in businesses that involve gambling or the buying and selling of intoxicants, living beings, or guns. Additionally, we should not make our living by means of fortune telling, palm reading, or the reading of feng shui.[10] These activities are not consistent with the observation of the precepts and contradict the teachings of conditioned co-arising.

The Venerable Yinguang demonstrated the importance of acquiring wealth in an ethical manner. For many years, he lived in Putuo Shan. During the Japanese invasion, one of his disciples invited him to come to Hong Kong to spread the Dharma. This student was a very successful businessman and wanted to offer a country house to the venerable for use as his residence. Though the venerable felt that the causes and conditions were ripe for him to leave Putuo Shan, he was reluctant to accept his student's invitation because he found out that he had made his fortune selling liquor. He declined the offer and told his student, "If you really want me to accept your offer, you have to stop selling liquor. The sale of liquor does not constitute right livelihood and is not consistent with the teachings of the Noble Eightfold Path. Therefore, I will not accept your offer."

When we abandon our ethics, the chance for a healthy relationship to wealth is disturbed and our affinity with others may be strained, as in the case above. Thus, if we plant the karmic seeds of wealth by giving alms and if we pursue our wealth in an ethical manner, the road to riches will be well within our reach.

Using wealth

While Buddhism teaches us not to be attached to the material world, it does not condemn the material world. Some people believe that one must be poor to be considered a cultivated or spiritual person. This is not true at all. Wealth by itself does not have any ethical value. It is the immoral pursuit of wealth, as well as its ill use, that causes difficulties and gives wealth its bad name. Money, if used properly, can be applied to the betterment of society and the nurturing of affinity. While it is true that money can be compared to a poisonous snake, it is equally true that it is a resource that we can use to spread the Dharma. For example, if we want to continually encourage new generations to engage in the work of spreading the Dharma, we need to provide a good education for the young. We need to set up schools. This takes money. We need to hire teachers; this also takes money. With adequate resources, we can even set up scholarships to provide educational opportunities for those who are unable to afford them on their own. Only with continual education can we ensure that the Buddha's teachings continue to shine in future generations. Thus, whether money is a poison or a tool, whether it contributes to harmony or discord, whether it builds affinity or causes distance, depends entirely on how it is used.

The *Wall Street Journal* once carried a story about a "modern-day bodhisattva" who used his wealth not for his own enjoyment but for the education of the young. This was a story about a surgeon, Dr. Joe McKibben, who donated twelve million dollars to the College of the Ozarks, a college known for offering its 1,500 mostly low-income students a tuition-free education in return for their labor. Some of you may think, "Well, surgeons make a lot of money. It is no skin off his back to make such a donation." What makes the story so touching are the personal sacrifices that Dr. McKibben had made throughout the years to amass his wealth. Though he was a surgeon and could live anywhere, he chose to live in a one-bedroom apartment in a modest neighborhood. He was a frugal man and would sometimes pick through the trash his neighbors threw out so that he might get some more use out of their discarded items. Taking his friend out to lunch meant going to a discount store and buying a two-for-one submarine sandwich. He would only drink water with his meals because he thought that ordering soft drinks was too wasteful. He was blessed with good fortune, and his investments yielded wonderful returns. The doctor was never married, and when he died, he left the majority of his assets to helping deserving students. Dr. McKibben gave us an inspiring example of how to use wealth prudently and in service to others.

In the sutras, the Buddha gives us some guidelines on how to manage our monetary assets. Our income can be skillfully used in a handful of ways. Our money can be invested in providing security for our parents, providing a comfortable living to our spouse and children, offering our children quality education, expanding our earning potential, saving for retirement, and making donations to help those in need. While this is not an exhaustive list of beneficial ways to use our money, these ideas can serve as guidelines for wise and considerate spending. The appropriate way to apportion wealth in these categories depends on each person's unique circumstances.

Measuring wealth
There are many ways to measure wealth. Some people measure wealth by how many material possessions they have or how much money they have in the bank. I look at wealth differently. I remember how destitute I was when I first arrived in Taiwan after fleeing China during the tumultuous years of World War II. All I had were the clogs on my feet and a few pieces of essential clothing. As I went from temple to temple looking for a permanent home, I was faced with rejection time and time again. During the war years, all the temples were hardly able to take care of their own residents, and they were most reluctant to accept a new monk into their ranks. There were days that I went without food. Finally, I arrived at a temple in the province of Hsinchu. The abbot of the temple, Venerable

Miaoguo, was compassionate and took me in. I was very grateful and was willing to help in whatever ways I could. In addition to teaching, I was also responsible for fetching water from the well for all to use. Every day, I had to fetch hundreds of pails of water, and I did it most willingly. Even though I did not possess many things, I felt most fortunate and content. When I went to the market before the break of dawn to buy vegetables for the day, the stars in the sky kept me company. Flowers and trees were there for me to enjoy. Roads were there for me to travel. I also had the opportunity to meet people from different walks of life. Though I possessed nothing, I had all the wealth the universe could offer me in the form of happy relationships with my surroundings and my newfound acquaintances. With such affinity, how could I ever consider myself poor?

The amount of money that one has does not determine one's happiness. True, the rich may not have to worry about where the next meal is coming from, but they can be burdened by social engagements and wearied by judging others' ulterior motives. Those with small incomes are not troubled by such problems. As long as they have their dignity and self-esteem, they can stand tall and be proud.

I want to share with you this parable. Once there was a wealthy businessman who lived in a penthouse with a breathtaking view of the city. He had a childhood friend who was poor but happy. This friend had a loving wife who adored him and greatly appreciated how hard he worked to provide for the family. The tycoon was a successful businessman and had to spend many evenings away from home socializing and finalizing business deals. He was quite envious of his friend's simple lifestyle and thought to himself, "What is the point of having all this money if I cannot enjoy it? My friend may be poor, but he is enjoying a wonderful life with his wife. Sometimes I wish my life could be more like his."

One day, someone told him, "If you want to be more like your friend, just give some of your money to him." He was tickled with the suggestion and decided to give his poor friend two hundred thousand dollars, a small fraction of what he had. The poor couple was ecstatic. They thought the money was the best thing that could happen to them. When night fell, they began to worry about how to safeguard their newfound wealth. Should they put it in the drawer? Someone might steal it. How about under the mattress? That did not sound like such a good hiding place either. Worried about their fortune, they hardly got a wink of sleep that night. After a few days, they began to argue about how best to use the money. The wife wanted to do one thing, while the husband wanted to do something different. Their fights almost destroyed their marriage. Upon reflection, they realized that all their problems had started when they were given the money. They decided to return the money to their tycoon friend instead.

This is, of course, a parable, but there is a valuable lesson here. Money can solve many problems, but it can also create many new ones. Our happiness depends more on our personal integrity and how we feel about ourselves, as well as the quality of our relationships, than on how much money we have in our bank accounts.

In the phenomenal world, everything is subject to impermanence. Wealth and poverty are no exceptions. Wealth can disappear, and people can go from rags to riches. In fact, the Buddha once said that our wealth does not belong to us but to five groups. The five groups are flood, fire, theft, a corrupt government, and prodigal children. Floods and fires can destroy in an instant what took years to build. We often read in newspapers how scam artists target older people and cheat them out of their life savings. Government policies and war can change the landscape of wealth, while spendthrift children can squander a fortune, however large. While we say, "This is mine," or "I possess this," the relationship we have with our wealth is actually much more tenuous.

We came into this world empty-handed, and we will leave the world the same way. The sutras say, "We cannot take anything with us; only karma shadows us everywhere." While this may sound obvious, many of us do not necessarily take it to heart.

The Buddha shows us by example a good way to relate to our wealth. He was just as happy with a simple robe as he was with a royal garment. He enjoyed the food that he collected from his alms rounds as much as the food that was offered to him when he was the guest of honor. He could sleep under a tree and yet was equally at ease in a royal palace. Sometimes he lived in solitude, and at other times he lived in the company of his followers. The Buddha was always at ease with his circumstances. The distinctions of rich and poor, coarse and fine, or fame and rejection had no bearing on his inner peace; this is true affinity with the material world.

If we measure wealth by how many material things we own, we will not feel content and satisfied. Desire is a bottomless pit and is often a game of relative wants and not absolute needs. It wasn't that long ago when only the very rich could afford conveniences that we all now take for granted, such as automobiles, books, and running water. If we had been alive at the turn of the last century, we would have thought that if we were to own a car, or if we were able to read whatever books we wanted, or if we could have had running water, we would not be in want of anything else. Now, when most of us are blessed with these modern-day conveniences, we want more. Regardless of how much we own, if we do not have inner peace, we will always desire more.

It is one thing to be poor in a monetary sense; it is quite another to be lacking spiritually. All too often we look outside of ourselves in our pursuit of wealth when the greatest wealth of all—our Buddha-nature—is right within us. The store of treasure within our hearts and minds is inexhaustible, and it is up to us to mine this internal wealth. If we know how to recognize and apply the treasure within, we are wealthy in the truest sense of the word.

❧ CHAPTER FIVE ❧

Living Affinity with Space and Time

IN THE LAST SECTION, we learned that the quality and depth of our relationship to the material world determines whether we wallow in the mindset of scarcity or celebrate the experience of abundance. Affinity with wealth also dictates whether we direct our monetary assets toward selfish or selfless endeavors. Space and time can be considered in a similar manner. The quality and depth of our relationship to space and time either shackles us to a puny and limiting idea of space and time, or frees us to encounter space and time without boundaries. Transforming how we view space and time, or, in other words, developing an affinity with space and time, also directs our intentions and actions toward helping others and toward the overall betterment of humankind.

Unfortunately, many of us do not yet realize our true capacity for understanding and relating to space and time, and therefore we remain trapped in our traditional and small perceptions. This can have a negative and confining influence on how we live our lives and whether or not we actualize our true potential to live freely and help others. For most living beings, time and space are just like the act of breathing: we breathe every moment yet are not conscious of this action. Depending on our individual makeup, we all have different understandings about time and space. For example, certain insects live for a day and are contented; human beings may live to seventy and are still not satisfied with this number of years. We all confine ourselves to our own limited slice of time and space, but really, a much more expansive and beneficial relationship with space and time is quite possible. Entering into this deeper affinity with space and time then changes our relationship to ourselves and to others in wonderful and unimaginable ways.

Although what we generally consider space is relatively minuscule, and although we generally consider time quite brief and fleeting, a limitless bounty of both is available to us when we pivot our angles of perception and regard both with a much more open mind and open heart. If we penetrate the ultimate truth of time and space, we can be liberated from the space defined by the four directions of north, south, west, and east, and emerge from the time cocoon of seconds, minutes, days, and months. In Buddhist thought, our very being "spans the three realms of existence" in terms of time, and "traverses the ten directions" in terms of space. What grand immensity! On the following pages, I will discuss ways in which we can view space and time differently, and consequently move from a perception of small and potentially limited dimensions to one that is both vast and compassionate. We will then be in the dimension of total freedom, and we will be able to experience what is described in the saying, "Clear, cool water everywhere; Prajna flowers every moment."

A. Living Affinity with Space
From the space outside us to the space inside us
Most of us have an idea of what constitutes the space outside us; it is the environment in which we live. This includes the house we live in, the city we live in, or even the world we live in. And just as we need to skillfully manage our relationship to others, to the environment, and to wealth, we also need to properly manage our relationship to the space outside us. For example, if we want to travel from place A to place B, we should have an idea about which route to use, what kind of transportation we need, how much time it requires, what we need to pack for the trip, and what potential problems we should anticipate. If we plan ahead, chances are we will have a wonderful trip. For more extensive trips, such as traveling around the world or journeying into space, more involved planning is called for, but the considerations are pretty much the same. Thus, if we expend the effort to analyze our circumstances and plan accordingly, we stand a fair chance of being able to manage the space outside us.

There are boundaries to what we call our external space. Regardless of how powerful or resourceful we are, the extent of our external space is still very limited. Some of you may disagree with this observation because we now have the ability to send people to the moon or to distant space stations. Yes, traveling to the moon or space stations is a reality, but the area we can cover is still just a small corner of our solar system. Our solar system is a minuscule fraction of our galaxy. There are millions upon millions of galaxies in the universe. Hard as we may try, in the grand scheme of the universe, the space in which we can leave our mark is as insignificant as a dust particle. Most of us spend our whole lifetime trying to amass as much space as possible. There is a Chinese saying that puts our conflict over space into perspective. It goes like this: "Having ten thousand acres of fertile land, yet sleeping only in an eight-foot space at night."

The space inside us is another story. It is without form and therefore without boundary. It is hard to visualize or comprehend. The Buddha told us that the space inside us is many times larger than the space outside us. One of the sutras says, "The mind encompasses the space of the universe, traversing realms as numerous as there are grains of sand." It is important to get to know the space inside us rather than becoming overly preoccupied with the space outside us. Before we go any further, let's clarify what we mean by internal space: we are speaking about our heart, and we should learn to let our heart grow. In Chinese literature, when someone has a big heart, we say that even boats can sail around in it. The Buddha told us that the immensity of the heart can encompass three thousand chiliocosms.[11] When we open up our heart, we can contain the whole universe within us.

When I first arrived in Taiwan in the 1940s, I was truly destitute in a material sense. Though I was penniless and my external situation was grim, I never felt in want of anything. The wealth that I found in nature was immeasurable. When I was down in spirit, the stars and moon in the sky kept me company. Flowers were there for me to enjoy; trees provided shade for me. Everything in nature gave me untold joy. When I felt the embrace and the expanse of the whole universe within me, how could I feel anything but rich and fulfilled? We have infinite spaciousness inside us, enough to hold the immensity of the cosmos; the universe is without, but the universe is also within. A true understanding of this capacity for inner abundance is key to finding ease and contentment regardless of our circumstances. Once, someone suggested to the father of Venerable Tzu Hui that he should do some traveling. He pointed to his heart and replied, "The whole universe is right here within my heart. Where else would I want to go?" How free!

So how do we let the spaciousness of our heart grow? The *Vimalakirti Sutra* teaches us the Dharma method of non-duality. When we open our heart, we are vast like the oceans, which welcome water from all tributaries, large and small, or like Mount Sumeru, which embraces earth of all kinds, coarse and fine. When we open our heart, disputes, politics, and power struggles will no longer affect us. We will be at ease wherever we find ourselves. Only when we have affinity with the space within us can we have affinity with the space outside us.

From the world ahead of us to the world behind us
While it is important that we know to forge ahead, it is even more important that we know to pause and look back. In fact, most of us only know how to forge ahead and do not realize that there is also a world of possibilities in the abundant space behind us. We tend to view the space of our lives from a single point of reference, forgetting that there is more than one direction to explore. When things are going our way, we charge ahead, seemingly unstoppable.

When we come to a brick wall, we stubbornly continue our forward motion, bringing much unnecessary suffering upon ourselves. The Buddha teaches that at any moment in life, there are two worlds for us to choose. One is the world ahead; the other is the world behind. We should develop a relationship with both of these worlds, without excluding either of them. When the time is right to charge ahead, we should charge ahead. When it is time to turn around, we should turn around. These two worlds are like our two hands; both are there for us to use. There is no need for us to go through life with one hand tied behind our back. There is a Buddhist poem that describes how we can move ahead by stepping backward. It goes like this:

> Green rice seedlings in hand,
> Planting rows in field.
> When lowering the head,
> Sky is seen in water.
> The path is nothing but
> Keeping body and mind clear, pristine.
> Ultimately, stepping backward is
> Stepping forward.

When we come to a precipice in the journey of life, we should remind ourselves of the old Chinese proverb and "Take a step back and think, [we will see] open seas and spacious sky." In this regard, we can look to nature for inspiration. Water is a perfect example. We all need water, and it is everywhere. When water flows downhill, it first picks up speed, then slows down as it reaches flat land. As it travels over the flat land, it meanders and automatically changes course when it hits obstructions. If we can learn to be like water and know when to change course, we will sail through life's obstacles and at the same time avoid unnecessary bruises.

Some people have said to me, "Your religion teaches people to refrain from smoking, drinking, and gambling. It takes all the fun out of life. Don't you feel restricted by that lifestyle?" We Buddhists refrain from smoking, drinking, and gambling because we see through the short-lived joy that such a lifestyle holds; we know enough to step back and change course. We would rather devote our energies to practicing the teachings, spreading the Dharma, and helping others. When we understand the vast spaciousness that surrounds us, and in fact *is* us, we are able to see countless opportunities for long-lived joy; how could we possibly feel restricted? When we truly understand that there will always be a world behind us, then we will know that we always have the choice to turn back, to change our course, to view life from a fresh perspective. We are not on an inevitable and unstoppable push forward—space is much more flexible than this. When we know to step back into the spaciousness that is always available to us, we will actually move ahead in life. When we embrace not only the world ahead of us but also the world behind us, then life is full of possibilities. How exhilarating!

From the phenomenal world to the transcendent world
So far, we have examined two ways of developing a new relationship to space by challenging our conventional outlook and enlarging our concept of the space available to us. We have moved from outside to inside, and from the world in front to the world behind. How do we move from the phenomenal world to the transcendent world? How

does this then transform and enlarge our relationship to space?

When we look at the phenomenal world around us, the world we see is covered with all kinds of colors and dotted with all different shapes—not unlike looking into a kaleidoscope. We all live in this world, and it is here we all pursue our hopes and dreams. How we live our lives in this world is entirely up to us. Some people see the world as a place to make money, others see it as a place for sharing with their loved ones, and still others see it as a place to make a name for themselves. It is very easy to get caught up in the phenomena of this world. Our delusions prevent us from seeing that all phenomena are only results of the combination of causes and conditions, without any independent nature of their own. The *Diamond Sutra* says, "All phenomena are illusory." If we understand this truth, we can transcend the phenomenal world and not be bound by it. We will still be participating in the phenomenal world, but we will exist beyond the conventional concept of space.

What is the transcendent world? Notice that the question is "what" and not "where," for the transcendent world is right here on the earth. Living in the transcendent world does not mean that we have to give up eating or sleeping. We will eat, sleep, and put on our clothes. The main difference is not to become preoccupied with the trifles of life. There is an old Chinese saying that can help us comprehend the meaning of the transcendent world. It goes like this: "Look at flowers and birds [unswayed] as a wooden carving would. Fear not the myriad things illusively surrounding us." When we live in this world of wild and plentiful phenomena without getting caught up in it, then our world becomes a transcendent world. We will have developed a more evolved relationship with space, and, in fact, we will have penetrated it.

While it is admirable for one to remove him- or herself from the rat race, it is even more admirable to work within it and remain true to oneself. Likewise, the lotus flower has always been the subject of admiration because it rises from the mud and yet remains pure. While it is easy to stay immaculate in a sterile environment, it is a lot more difficult to remain clean in a contaminated setting. For Buddhists, choosing to retreat in isolation is not the supreme form of cultivation, but to remain unswayed when surrounded by temptation is. Thus we say, "The most cultivated cultivate in the midst of the crowd." We have special admiration for those who practice the Dharma amidst the hustle and bustle of life. Throughout history, there have been many such examples for us to learn from. The Chinese poet Tao Yuanming wrote, "Live amongst the people, yet hear not the bustle of horses and carriages." Vimalakirti "lived in a family, but was unattached to the three realms of existence. He lived with a wife, but his practice was always impeccable." Venerable Yi-hsiu, a respected monk of his time, was another good example. Once while he was out traveling with his disciple, he saw a woman by the bank of a swift-flowing river, wondering how she would cross to the other side. The elder offered to carry her across on his back. In the old days in China, physical contact between men and women was strictly forbidden. His disciple, horrified that his teacher would have such contact with a woman, remained sullen for a whole month. When the elder found out what was bothering his student, he told his student, "I've already forgotten the whole incident. I only carried the woman across, but you have been carrying her in your mind for a whole month." Such carefree living is described by the saying, "Pass through a grove of flowers without a single leaf clinging to the body." When we see through the illusion of the phenomenal world and do not become attached to anything, then we are living transcendentally. This transcendental relationship to the world is the crux of living affinity with the space around us.

In the last three sections, we talked about how to experience the space inside us, how to see the world behind us, and how to live transcendentally. When we view space through the Buddha's teachings, we will begin to develop a different relationship with the space of life. Our focus will move from outside inward, from the world ahead to the world behind, from the phenomenal to the transcendental. In this way, our space of life becomes infinitely larger and contains more joy and potential than we ever thought possible.

B. Living Affinity with Time

Like our relationship to space, our relationship to time can also enlarge to one of immense and beneficial proportions. We can have a foolish relationship with time or a wise one, a wasteful relationship or one in which productivity increases a thousandfold, a relationship that promotes affinity with others or one that hinders it, a relationship that is based only on brevity or one that embraces eternity.

One of the sutras says, "We live from breath to breath." This saying reminds us of the brevity and impermanence of life. Even though the mythical Peng Zu might have lived for eight hundred years and the life span of celestial beings extends to tens of thousands of years, such life spans when viewed in the context of eternity are as fleeting as the morning dew. Each one of us should treasure the time we have and use it wisely. We should use our limited time to enrich our lives and live life to its fullest meaning, while gaining an understanding that, ultimately, time has no beginning and no ending at all. It is entirely possible to establish a relationship with time in which we are never struggling against it, only living in utmost harmony with it and maximizing its use for the benefit of all beings. We will explore how to build this kind of affinity with time in the following three points.

Use every bit of time
Some of us live to seventy, while others may live to be a hundred. The limited time we have in this world is often diminished by all kinds of necessary activities we must do to stay alive. Because of these activities, a twenty-four hour day is often chopped up into bits and pieces. We eat, sleep, work at our jobs, and work around the house; before we know it, another day is over. To prepare food, we have to first buy it, then cook it, and only then consume it. Even if we go out to eat, we still have to travel to a restaurant, wait to be served, and then consume the food. Sleeping also takes up a lot of our time. First, we have to tidy our beds, and then we sometimes toss and turn before falling asleep. While we may or may not enjoy eating or sleeping, we still must engage in these activities. There is just no getting around it. If we take the limited years we have and deduct from them the time we spend on eating, sleeping, traveling from place to place, waiting in lines, cleaning ourselves, and going to the bathroom, how much time would we have left? On top of this, if we take away the years we were

young and the time we will spend debilitated by old age, there is really not that much time left to apply ourselves to the betterment of humankind. The prime years of our lives are truly limited and brief.

In this day and age of cell phones and beepers, time seems to pass and life appears to move at an incredible pace. People often try to "multi-task," completing several chores at the same moment in an attempt to "save time." With the advent of pagers, faxes, and wireless telephones, the nine-to-five workday is a thing of the past. Life is so jam-packed with deadlines and schedules that every second counts. It is easy for us to lose sight of our purpose and forget why we busied ourselves in the first place. Some people say it is a blessing to be busy and feel needed, but we have to be careful that we are preoccupied for the right reasons. Some people only focus on themselves and cannot give others the time of day. Others give their jobs their all and neglect their own family. In today's fast-paced society, if we don't know how to make use of every bit of time, we will find ourselves always struggling for more. With a new perspective on time, we can eliminate this struggle and skillfully adapt to a hectic lifestyle. It is quite important for us to use our time wisely.

Given how fragmented our days and years are and knowing how important it is for us to use every bit of our time, how do we do so? I often encourage people to make use of every bit of time. In the case of young students, I advise them to make use of the fifteen minutes they have here and there to read a book, write in a journal, or review a chapter. Why waste time chatting or watching television? You can recite the name of the Buddha while you are cleaning or cooking. You can also recite the name of

Amitabha while you are waiting for the bus or commuting to your workplace. This is an excellent practice to begin at a young age, for society moves at a rapid pace, and elderly people often find themselves withdrawing, as they age. While there is hardly enough time to do everything when we are young, the opposite is true when old age sets in. Chanting the Buddha's name in solitude when even a modicum of physical activity is difficult or unfeasible is an excellent way for a senior citizen to spend time. I also suggest that we all develop the habit of reading when we are still young. Then, when we are less mobile, we can always sit back with a good book. We have to keep the mind young by keeping it busy and engaged. When our eyes are tired, we can recite the Buddha's name. When we are mindful of Buddha, Buddha will always be in our hearts.

There is an old Chinese saying that we can use as our guide: "Say one less sentence; recite one more time the name of Amitabha Buddha." The flip side of this is also captured by another common Chinese saying, "Diseases enter in through the mouth; problems come out from the mouth." When we chat with our friends and do not think about what we are saying, we can easily say something that offends them without our even realizing it. So, when we have a moment of free time, we should make use of it to recite the name of Amitabha Buddha or to contemplate the splendid appearance of the Buddha. And conversely, when we are busy, we can recite Amitabha's name to calm our minds. Amitabha stands for "infinite light" and "infinite life," a good anchor in the ups and downs of life. This is not only a way to keep from offending others inadvertently; it is also an effortless way to practice. This is truly a win-win situation. When we are constantly mindful of the Buddha, we will be at peace with whatever we are doing. When we can make use of the fragmented time we have, our practice will be benefited as well.

When we began to build Fo Guang Shan Temple in Taiwan many years ago, others were skeptical and asked me, "Are you an architect? What do you know about building houses? Are you a trained educator? What do you know about running schools?" I would tell those people that my biggest secret is that I know how to use my time. Even though I am not an architect or a trained educator, I have traveled to many places and seen many houses. I often put myself in the shoes of the building contractor and imagined what I would do if I were building such-and-such a house. When I was still in school, I would often think about what I would do differently if I were running the school. When we began building Fo Guang Shan Temple, I already had an idea of what I wanted to do, and through using my time wisely, everything just fell into place. I was in tune with my capacity—the capacity that everyone has—to accomplish great things in the face of fleeting time.

Unfortunately, when I look around, I see a lot of people squandering their time. It is unlikely that someone who doesn't know how to utilize his or her time will ever achieve anything remarkable. There is an art to managing time. We have to apportion our time so that we know how to balance the demands of material and spiritual needs. We have to look out for ourselves, yet we should also have others' well-being in mind. We must work for the present as well as for the future. If we can strike a balance in all these areas, then we are managing our time well and we will not have squandered a precious moment of it.

Seize the present moment

The passing of time is inevitable and merciless. If we are not watchful, time slips by us without a trace, like a thin veil of fog or columns of clouds in the sky. We have to seize the present moment, for time waits for no one. If we wait for things to happen, we often end up sitting idly by. We should treasure the limited years we have in this life and apply ourselves to living the best we can. We should work to better ourselves, for we do not want to look back when we are old and wish that our lives had been different.

Once, there were two men from Szechwan; both of them wanted to make a pilgrimage to the Guanyin Temple of Putuo Shan. One man wanted to wait until he had saved up enough money to hire a boat so that he could travel by sea to the shores of Putuo Shan. The other man was a poor man, but he wanted to start right away. He decided to travel to Putuo Shan on foot, asking for alms along the way. After a while, the poor man returned while the other man had yet to hire a boat, let alone start out on the pilgrimage.

The moral of the story is that we should not spend our lives waiting for things to happen; instead, we should seize the present moment and make things happen. As long as we have the ability to do good, we should act as soon as an opportunity presents itself. In fact, we can be proactive with our time and actually create opportunities to do good. We do not want to have to look back and think about what could have been if only we hadn't procrastinated. When we are young, we should make use of our youth and apply ourselves. We do not want to wait till our hair is all gray to realize that we have wasted our youth. If we are wise, we will not romanticize the past or fantasize about the future; we will simply live in the present, making the best use of our time.

The following parable illustrates that there are two kinds of time. Once there was an old man whose hair was all white, and a few of his teeth were missing. Someone asked him, "Mister, how old are you?"

"Four," answered the elderly gentleman.

The person was puzzled and said, "You must be kidding. Judging from your gray hair, you cannot possibly be four. If I have to guess, I'd say you are about seventy or eighty years old."

The elderly gentleman continued, "Let me explain. On a calendar basis, I am eighty years old, but all my life I had been fumbling along, waiting for things to happen to me. I only started *truly* living about four years ago when I became interested in Buddhism. In these four years, I've actively pursued the truth about life and the universe. Now I work, not for myself, but for others."

The first kind of time is when we just sit around waiting for things to happen. The second kind of time is when we actively try to make things happen. These are two very different kinds of time. The former demonstrates a foolish and wasteful relationship with time, while the latter shows a wise and advantageous relationship with time.

The sands of time disappear one grain at a time, and before long, we wonder where the years have gone. We should use the time we have to make whatever contributions we can. When we first began to build Fo Guang Shan Temple in Taiwan, the area we had chosen was a remote and barren piece of land. Some people questioned why we were "wasting" our time. With determination and the help of many faithful devotees, we finally completed what we had started and turned a vision into a reality. Imagine: If we had not started when we did or if we had decided to wait for a better location, Fo Guang Shan might not be where it is today. If we had chosen a different relationship with time—one of scarcity instead of abundance—than surely we could not have accomplished our goal. We would not have had the confidence that there was enough time to complete such a massive project. But if we develop our affinity with time, and if we use time to create rather than to wait, then we can turn dreams into reality. Whenever we dedicate ourselves to serving others, our time is well spent.

Realize eternity through the brevity of life
If we only focus on how limited our life is, we will begin to think that life is dull and lacks possibilities. We will constantly be hindered by perceived boundaries and will frequently miss opportunities to help others and do good in the world. On the contrary, if we realize that the true span of our life is everlasting, then life becomes a lot more interesting and is suddenly rich with possibilities. Some of you may say that since we all will die one day it is impossible to say that life is everlasting. But it is only when we view life as merely the existence of the physical body that we regard our life span as limited to only a few decades. We tend to think that our time begins when we are born and ends when we die. Because of our tunnel vision and our attachment to the phenomenal world, we do not realize that our being is much larger than this physical manifestation. However, when we look at existence in the context of the cycle of rebirth, we have a long history and an unbounded future. Our physical body is like a house. When the house is beyond repair, we move on to a new

one. When our bodies grow old and die, we move into a new body. Of course, the kind of body we take up will depend on our cumulative good and bad karma.

If we can break out of our small mindset, we will see that death is, in fact, the beginning of another life. According to the Buddha's teachings, death is not the final chapter of life; it merely marks the end of one life and the beginning of another. The Buddha teaches us that life is without beginning and without end. Life is the culmination of causes and conditions, and as such it is continually changing. Like the water in a fast-running river, it is never the same water. As soon as some water flows away, more comes to take its place. This impermanence is an inherent characteristic of the phenomenal world. Look around you. We go through birth, aging, and death. Likewise, the inanimate world is marked with becoming, existing, and ceasing. The sutras say: "Mount Sumeru may be huge and tall, yet it will disappear one day. Despite the great depths of the sea, it will become dry when its time is up. Though the sun and moon shine bright, they will cease to exist before long. The great earth may be strong and holds all there is, but when the fire of karma burns at the end of the kalpa, it, too, cannot escape impermanence." When we see this truth, we will no longer fear death and rebirth. We will understand that the process of death and rebirth, as previously mentioned, is like moving from one house to the next.

While our form, or our "house," may be different for each rebirth, our Buddha-nature remains the same. Unfortunately, many of us do not know our Buddha-nature, our true self. As we course through the cycles of rebirth, we become attached to the impermanent, non-self

self and lose touch with our Buddha-nature. In Buddhist literature, there is a story that speaks of our ignorance. One time, a monk passed by a family's home on his alms round. It so happened that the family was busy celebrating a wedding, and no one paid him any attention. The monk looked around and sighed,

> Cows, sheep, animals sitting at table;
> Grandmother from a past life is now the bride.
> Beating drum in hall: hitting grandpa's skin;
> Cooking in pots the aunts.

The monk felt a sense of pity for the sentient beings who could not see impermanence and did not understand existence in the context of rebirth. Their actions suggested that they had no affinity with universal life—they were unaware of their connection to the infinite continuum of existence. Unbeknownst to them, the animals that were being cooked in the kitchen pots were the aunts of previous lives. The guests of the wedding had been cows and sheep in their previous lives. The bride had been in fact the groom's grandmother in a previous lifetime.

If we could look into the past and future, we would realize that many of the myriad relationships in this world are both pitiful and laughable because they are not viewed in the context of the eternal continuity of time and life or the endless cycle of rebirth. *The Inspiration to Pledge Our Bodhicitta* speaks of two such examples: "Whipping the mule until it bleeds, who knows of my mother's sorrow? Taking the animal to be slaughtered, how do I know of your father's pain?" There is a story behind these two lines. Once there was a family who had a mule. For many years, the family used the mule to pull produce to the market. When the mule grew old, it was no longer strong enough to pull the cartloads of produce. The mule's owner thought that he could get some more use out of it if only he could show the mule who the master was. Every day he whipped the mule so that it would work harder. One night, he dreamed of the mule appearing before him in human form, pleading with him, "In your previous life, I was your mother. I was not a good mother and neglected you. As a result, I was reborn as a mule to repay my debt to you. For the last twenty years, I helped you transport produce to the market. Now that I am old and weak, I can no longer work as I did before. Please have pity on me and spare me your whipping." When the man woke up, he was ashamed that he had been so cruel, so he took the mule to a nearby temple and allowed it to live out its days in peace. He had gained a greater understanding about the nature of life and death, the cycle of rebirth, and the continuity of life. With a new perception of how life and death occur within the context of unbounded time, he became more skilled at offering compassion to his fellow beings.

Let's take the earlier rebirth analogy of moving into a new house a step further. If we have been putting money away while living in our current house, then we can afford to move to a nicer, bigger house when the current one starts to fall apart. If we have not been putting money away, then, when it is time to move, we'll have no choice but to move down to a smaller house. Thus, while our life span is limited, we should use our time wisely to act compassionately and do good. By steadfastly practicing during this brief existence, we will undergo a favorable rebirth when it is time for us to depart this body. Thus,

Buddhists do not fear death, and we do not look at death as the final chapter of life.

So how do we use our limited time to do good and bring about infinite value? Let me tell you a story. Once, there was an elderly gentleman who wanted to plant a peach tree. As he was laboring to plant the small peach tree, a young man passed by. The young man struck up a conversation with the elderly man and asked, "Sir, are you sure you want to spend so much energy on planting this tree? You may not live to see it grow, let alone enjoy its fruit. Is this not a waste?"

The old man stood up and wiped off his sweat. With his dry, crackling voice, he looked at the young man and, in a serious tone, replied, "You are too young to understand the meaning of life. I want to plant this tree not for myself. Though I may not live to see it bear fruit, my sons will get to enjoy its shade, and my grandchildren will enjoy its fruit. How can you say this is a waste?"

The young man was moved by the profound insight of the elderly gentleman. The older man knew that later generations would enjoy the fruits of the labor of earlier generations, and so he acted accordingly. We should not look at life just as the limited span of one person's life; we should look at the larger life of the universe. While a person's life may only span a limited number of years, its value is everlasting. The continuity of life through one person to another is not unlike the process of spreading fire from one log to another. While the fire of the second log is not the same as the fire of the first log, it represents a continuation of the fire from the first log. In a similar way, from one being to another, we can see the continuity of life. Affinity also transcends one's life span—its energy flows through life's continuity and, by building affinity in our lifetime, we will pass it along to the next generation.

Given that we all play linking roles in this continuum of life, how are we to contribute to this larger life? Some people contribute through politics, others through their writing, still others through their examples. While these are all worthwhile contributions, Buddhism teaches us a more complete and supreme way. Buddhism teaches that when we discover our own Dharmakaya, then we have found our own eternity. Dharmakaya is everywhere and everlasting. Our great teacher, Sakyamuni Buddha, is a great example of one who found eternity in the Dharmakaya. Though the Blessed One entered nirvana over twenty-five hundred years ago, the Dharmakaya of the Buddha is still here with us. This is the meaning of eternity in life and the ultimate example of affinity with time.

❧ CHAPTER SIX ❧

Living Affinity with the Spiritual
Aspect of Life

I WISH TO CLOSE this book by exploring an all-important and all-encompassing relationship—our relationship to the spiritual aspect of life. Human beings are spiritual beings, and our mind and heart may lie dormant, small, and deluded if we do not tend to this aspect of ourselves. We all have a desire to know ourselves and live our lives with great joy. We want to reveal the original purity of our true nature so that we are no longer encumbered by false desires, perceptions, and habits. True knowledge about own nature and about the nature of life will unfold as we persevere in developing our inner lives; we will discover spiritual affinity.

As we cultivate spiritual affinity, we will discover that our true nature is in fact living affinity. Our true nature is one of ultimate harmony and accord, where no distinctions, discriminations, separateness, or divisions exist. And, because all beings share this nature, we are already living affinity with all phenomena. Although we discuss "creating" and "building" affinity with others, the environment, material possessions, and so forth, what we are actually saying is that we are unfolding the natural affinity that always was and always will be. All beings already *are* this inherent and unblemished affinity; it is up to us to recognize it and live it. An engaged spiritual practice can help us to do this.

To assist you in cultivating a deeper spiritual practice, I wish to cover several topics that will help you further understand the Buddha's teachings regarding spiritual development. The following discussion will address these questions: What does the Buddha teach regarding spiritual needs? What is right understanding? How should I perceive myself? What do I do if I make mistakes along the path? How do I stay faithful to my practice? How do I live ethically? As we contemplate these questions and probe deeper and deeper for answers, we will begin to dismantle the barriers and dissolve the mindsets that keep us from knowing our true nature and actualizing *living affinity*.

The Noble Eightfold Path and right understanding

The Buddha teaches the Noble Eightfold Path, which is the most comprehensive set of teachings regarding spiritual development. The Path is not unlike a road map for the journey of life. It is an atlas that guides us through our relationships with everything we have explored thus far: community, friendship, love, material possessions, wealth, environments, space, and time. Without this road map, we may feel confused, or even overwhelmed, by the twists and turns we encounter. Only when we have the road map in hand can we have an idea of where we have been or where we are going.

What are the aspects of the Noble Eightfold Path? They are: right understanding, right thought, right speech, right action, right livelihood, right effort, right mindfulness, and right concentration. Of these eight practices, right understanding precedes the others and serves as the foundation. The word "right" here does not have the connotation of "right or wrong." Right understanding can also be translated as full or wholesome understanding. Right understanding entails the internalization of the reality of rebirth and karma and its effects, as well as the nature of wholesome or unwholesome actions, speech, and thought. Having right understanding is like having the appropriate settings when taking pictures with a manual camera. If the focal length and aperture of the lens are not set correctly, then the pictures will be blurry. If we do not have right understanding, then we will not be able to see the truth regarding worldly phenomena or the workings of life and the universe. We will not have the right state of mind for developing pure affinities and wholesome relationships—including our relationship to and perception of ourselves as we seek to reveal our true nature, the ultimate affinity.

We all say, "I feel that...," or "I believe that...," or "My opinion is...." We all differ in the way we see things, for our assessment of the world is colored by our past experiences and karma. We are constantly viewing through the eyes of distinction, perceiving a big divide between happiness and sorrow, good times and bad times, easy and difficult, have and have not, likes and dislikes, self and others, and even life and death. We go to great lengths to avoid what we view as painful, and we are quickly drawn to what we perceive as pleasurable. Our discriminatory perceptions cause us great suffering, keep us divided, and enshroud inherent affinity. Right now, we all have our own individual biases; only a fully enlightened Buddha continually sees things as they truly are. For the Buddha, there are no dualities, and therefore there is never an instance when one thing is "versus" another. The Buddha teaches us that right understanding is to see the truth of all things, to comprehend worldly phenomena as they are, to see things in their true state and to experience for ourselves the essence of the Dharma. This understanding helps us to be at ease with the circumstances in which we find ourselves and guides us to the revelation of our true nature. How can we be ill at ease if we tap into this natural and inherent affinity?

Selflessness

Some Buddhists are lacking in right understanding about "self." Earlier, we discussed transforming our perception of "self and others." It is equally important to explore our sense of self, for an erroneous perception of self is always a cause of our suffering and a hindrance to unimpeded cultivation and uninhibited affinity. It is said in the sutras, "The cause of our suffering lies in the presence of the physical body." What this means is that the root cause of our suffering lies in our attachment to this impermanent, non-substantial body we call "self" and our error of mistaking it for our true self. The phenomenal self is actually nothing more than the combination of the five aggregates: form, feeling, perception, mental formation, and consciousness. Because of the five aggregates, we have discrimination, resulting in attachment and aversion. The sutras also say that human beings are plagued by eighty-four thousand vexations and agitations, commonly referred to as "afflictions" in Buddhist texts. These afflictions, which are like bandits, are led by the three main culprits of greed, anger, and ignorance. The commander-in-chief of these three culprits is the notion[12] of self.

How can we guard against the invasion of these bandits? The answer lies in "selflessness," which is essentially eliminating the commander-in-chief of the bandits. When we speak of selflessness in Buddhism, we are not talking about non-existence or the termination of life. The body reconstitutes after death in a new rebirth and cannot be eliminated by physical means. The selflessness that we speak of is letting go of the notion of self. If we can see that what we normally call the self is nothing more than the result of the five aggregates coming together and is inherently empty in nature, we would not cling to the notion of self so tightly. Let me illustrate this point with the following story.

Once there was a man who took a wrong turn on his way back home from a trip. As the night set in, he found shelter in a little abandoned house by the roadside. Not long after he settled down, he saw a ghost about to enter the house, hauling a corpse behind him. Before he had time to take cover, an even larger ghost appeared at the door. Without so much as a word, the larger ghost tried to wrestle the corpse from the first ghost. The traveler was scared out of his wits and unknowingly let out a squeal. The big ghost heard the noise and said, "Someone is hiding in the house. Let us ask this person who is the rightful owner of the corpse."

Meanwhile, the little ghost spotted the man and grabbed him by the collar. He asked the traveler, "Tell the truth. Who did you see hauling the corpse in the first place?"

The man thought to himself, "If I speak the truth, the big ghost will not be too pleased with me. If I lie, I will anger the little ghost and create bad karma for myself. Either way, I am in big trouble. I may as well speak the truth."

The man described what he had seen, which angered the big ghost tremendously. The big ghost tore off the man's left arm and swallowed it. The little ghost felt sorry for the man and wanted to help. He tore the left arm off the corpse and transplanted it onto the man. This angered the big ghost even more, and he then tore off the man's right arm. The little ghost again replaced the missing arm with one from the corpse. The same thing happened to the man's legs and head. After a lot of commotion, both ghosts left in a huff. The man, who was in a state of shock, asked himself, "Who am I? These are not my limbs. This is not my head."

With advances in medicine, all kinds of organ transplants are now possible. In fact, scientists are looking into cloning human organs or using organs from other species for transplants. In the age of cloning and organ transplants, how do we define the self? Even twenty-five hundred years ago, the Buddha taught us to see the physical body as the combination of the five aggregates and as being empty in nature. When we truly understand the meaning of this, we will not be attached to the form and feeling of the physical body. When we fail to understand this, we set ourselves up for many disappointments and cut ourselves off from a profound experience of universal affinity.

We all have our share of headaches and heartaches. Physically, we all have to face aging, sickness, and death. Mentally, we have to deal with problems arising from greed, anger, and ignorance. The Chinese have a saying that aptly describes our predicament: "Heaven and hell sometimes end; the threads of sorrow continue forever." Our vexation and agitation are as deep as the dark, blue sea and as dense as the trees in the wild. These anxieties are also the driving force that propels us from one rebirth to another.

Our anxieties, however numerous and varied, all stem from one cause—the attachment to self. Because of this attachment, we look at the world from a singular view-point, stopping ourselves from an all-encompassing and all-embracing way of living. This exclusive perception creates many problems for ourselves and others. The three poisons of greed, anger, and ignorance all originate from this attachment. To root out all our headaches and heartaches, we have to do so at the source. In other words, we have to realize that "self" is merely a construct of our minds and break free from the oppression of the three poisons. Wang Yangming, a famous Confucian scholar of the Ming Dynasty, once said, "To catch the bandit in the hills is easy, to arrest the thief in ourselves is tough." Fortunately, the Buddha teaches us what we should do. "Work diligently on discipline, meditative concentration, and wisdom; extinguish the fires of greed, anger, and ignorance." Because of our deep-rooted attachment to the notion of self, we can only see reality through this narrow periscope and often act as though we were the center of the universe. The discipline of upholding the precepts helps us refrain from violating others' rights. It is a good countermeasure against greed. Meditative concentration helps us stay centered when facing hostility. Staying calm can also help us carefully assess a difficult situation and make the right decision. Meditative concentration reveals wisdom so that we can see through our delusion. The wisdom we speak of here is transcendental wisdom and is not the same as worldly knowledge. Transcendental wisdom is the understanding of emptiness and the law of conditionality. Wisdom guides our actions so that we do not end up habitually reacting to our emotions.

Many of us have heard of the saying, "Do no evil, speak no evil, and hear no evil." This is a good start. When we are vigilant at the three doors of karma—speech, actions, and thoughts—we are removing the conditions for the three poisons to grow. Our senses can be very troublesome things. Because of our sensory discriminations, we develop preferences and aversions, many of them quite arbitrary and meaningless. Instead of looking for affirmation or definition of who we are from outside of ourselves, we should look within ourselves. In this way, we see that a lot of our sorrows are quite self-inflicted and unnecessary.

Repentance and the three doors of karma
While we can understand that doing no evil, speaking no evil, and hearing no evil create the ideal conditions for revealing our pure, original nature, none of us goes through life with a perfect record. We all make mistakes in

deed, speech, and thought, causing ourselves and others misery and disrupting the natural flow of affinity in our relationships. Unwholesome conduct also creates bad karma. Part of developing spiritually is being able to recognize these occasions and make amends. Buddhism places a great deal of emphasis on continually reflecting on the three doors of karma and pondering with a sense of remorse the ill we have caused. Unwholesome behavior does not need to be a permanent impediment to our spiritual cultivation. If we handle these unfortunate circumstances with integrity and sincerity, we can continue our progress in cultivation, even while the retribution of karma is inevitable. Repentance is a gateway into the Dharma and has a profound impact on our practice. There is a Buddhist saying that captures the power of repentance well: "Lay down the slaying knife; immediately become a Buddha." Without repentance, we remain shackled to our previous wrongdoings and it is more difficult to turn ourselves around and begin to create good karma, instead of continuing to create bad karma.

Through repentance we are "washed clean" of our mistakes. When our clothes are dirty, we wash them to get rid of the dirt. When our bodies are filthy, a bath helps us feel clean again. When children do something wrong, we want them to be honest about their mistakes and make amends. Likewise, when we make mistakes, we have to be remorseful. This following gatha is often recited in repentance services to help us repent of our wrongdoings:

All the wrongs I have committed in the past
Arise from beginningless greed, anger, and ignorance.

What I have committed with my body, speech, and
  thought,
All these I now repent.

In this age of laying blame, we like to think of our
mistakes as the result of irresistible temptations, moments
of mental weakness, the effect of growing up in a dysfunc-
tional family, or the demands of making ends meet. The
Buddha teaches us that our unwholesome karma is the
result of greed, anger, and ignorance from time without
beginning. Being born in this day and age does not help,
either. Modern life is so hectic that civility is a rare
commodity. Many people have a short fuse, and obscenity
is on the rise.

What is repentance? How should we repent? The
sutras give us some guidelines. First, we have to be honest
about our mistakes and be determined not to repeat them.
It is not enough to admit our wrongs privately; we need to
confess openly to the Buddha or to someone who can
guide us. We should also be willing to accept the conse-
quences of our actions. Second, we should sincerely ask
the Buddhas and bodhisattvas for strength so that we do
not make the same mistakes again. Avalokitesvara
Bodhisattva exudes compassion and helps those who
repent of their unwholesome karma. The *Chapter of
Universal Gateway* says, "Regardless of their guilt or inno-
cence, when someone bound and shackled recites the
name of Avalokitesvara, the shackles will break open. True
freedom will be realized." A field that is not cultivated will
not yield a harvest. If the field is then tilled and fertilized,
crops will grow and weeds will not take root. In a similar
way, someone who is mindful of the Buddhas and

bodhisattvas will be able to mitigate the ripening of unwholesome karma.

Let's explore karma further. On one level of understanding, our karmas are created by our body, speech, and thought. If we investigate this a bit further, we come to see that even unwholesome karma is empty and without a self-nature. In repentance, we see into the emptiness of unwholesome karma, and the original luster of our pure nature is restored. The sutras say:

> When defilements arise, clarify deluded mind.
> When delusion ceases, defilement also dies.
> Delusions cleared, defilements disappear—both
>   are completely empty.
> This is called true repentance.

As we can see from this stanza, repentance here has a different dimension than the normal use of the word. Repentance is more than feeling sorry for what we have done. Repentance also involves clarifying deluded thought. When we see the emptiness of our delusion, we also see the emptiness of unwholesome karma. In so doing, we see things as they truly are. Hell is "recognized"[13] as heaven, affliction is recognized as bodhi, defilement is recognized as purity, our world is recognized as a pure land, and aversion is recognized as affinity.

In addition to repentance, we also have to vow to do good. The four universal vows are like signposts to a pure land:

> To aid all living beings without limit,
> To sever all delusion without end,

To master all Dharma methods and means
   however numerous,
To realize the supreme Buddha way.

If we all learn to be vigilant in guarding the three
doors of karma and are repentant of the harm we've
caused, then we stand a better chance of creating more
good karma than bad and revealing our true nature instead
of covering it up. One of the sutras tells us, "Fear not the
stir of delusions; fear, though, the delay of awareness."
When our delusions cause us to act unwholesomely, we
should immediately recognize them and repent of our
actions. What is most tragic is when we do not see our
faults and continue to make the same mistakes over and
over again. If we mistakenly walk into a swamp, we still
can be saved if we quickly turn around and walk away. If,
however, we stubbornly persist in the same course of
action, we will be beyond hope of being rescued.

Ethical living
The last topic that I want to cover is ethical living. This is
another very important subject related to cultivating spiritual affinity. While we may experience deep and profound
spiritual progress, if our actions do not reflect this inner
affinity, than our development means very little. Our
behavior must manifest the spiritual transformation that is
happening within us; in other words, our ethics must be
intact. When we abandon our ethics, we tarnish our spiritual affinity, and, ultimately, the quality of our lives is
compromised. Unethical behavior not only causes our
internal affinity to falter, but it also adversely affects our
external relationships, causing problems such as losing our

friends, harming our loved ones, or getting fired from our job. In the journey of life, I hope that we all lead our lives ethically. However, the meaning of ethics is not always easily understood or defined. What do I mean by ethical living? The heart of ethical living is practicing what we believe in and following through with our intentions. Let me try to explain this further with some examples that will point us in the direction of living our lives ethically.

Practice the Buddha's teachings
Once we understand the Buddha's teachings, we need to put them into practice and experience them for ourselves. Understanding the teachings without practicing them renders them meaningless and causes our spiritual development to stagnate. The Buddha teaches us to be compassionate, but some Buddhists maintain their jealous and hateful ways. The Buddha teaches us to give alms, but some Buddhists still cannot practice giving with grace and joy in their hearts. The Buddha teaches us to practice right livelihood, but some Buddhists choose to ignore this teaching.

When the Buddha was alive, there was an elder by the name of Sudatta. He was a most generous man and took the Buddha's teachings to heart. He was often referred to as Anathapindada, which literally means one who gives to widows and orphans. He wanted to construct a monastery and invite the Buddha to preach in his hometown, but the land which he had in mind was owned by Prince Jeta. He wanted to buy the land from the prince and even agreed to pave the land with gold in order to convince the prince of his determination to convert the land into a sanctuary for spreading the Dharma. This is the story behind the origin of the Jetavana Monastery, a place where the Buddha often stayed when preaching the Dharma up in the northern areas of ancient India. Sudatta offers a good example of one who practices what he believes in.

Sudatta wanted his whole family to live in accordance with the Buddha's teachings, but one of his daughters-in-law was an arrogant woman. She was beautiful but conceited. Because of her beauty, she was quite haughty and was often disrespectful and condescending to her family and friends, thereby jeopardizing her relationships. Sudatta tried to show her the error of her ways on many occasions, but he met with little success. In frustration, he went to the Buddha for help. The Buddha then sat down with Sudatta's daughter-in-law and explained the Dharma to her. She was deeply moved by the Buddha's teachings and decided to change her ways. She vowed to uphold the precepts and to live in accordance with the Dharma.

Vimalakirti is another excellent example of one who lived and practiced the teachings. He led a householder's life, but he maintained an impeccable practice. He was very wealthy, but he was not attached to material riches. Vimalakirti is someone whom we all should strive to emulate.

Ethical living as exemplified by cultivated monks and everyday heroes

Like Sudatta and Vimalakirti, there were, and still are, many cultivated monks throughout the history of Chinese Buddhism who have shown the depth of their convictions through their actions. Venerable Xinxing of the Sui Dynasty once made his home on the steep face of a mountain. When he was asked why he had chosen such an inconvenient spot to live, he answered that he was needed there. The road adjacent to where he lived was so narrow that there was not enough room for two carts to pass each other. Every day, after his morning devotions, he would proceed to the road to help those who were stuck, because of opposing traffic, to back up their carts. In this way, he grounded the core of his practice, as well as this mental well-being and happiness, in helping others.

The Chan master Baizhang of the Tang Dynasty believed in the value of work. He would say, "A day without work is a day without food." Every day he would work before eating. In his later years, when his health was failing, he still insisted on working every day. His disciples could not bear to see him labor, so they hid all his tools. When the master could not find his tools to start his day's work, he actually refused to eat for that day. Seeing his conviction, his disciples had no choice but to hand him back his tools. Through his unwavering commitment to work, the master manifested his principles in his conduct. He found great joy in this practice.

We do not have to look far into history to find people who have strong convictions in doing what they believe is the right and most beneficial thing to do. There are many modern-day heroes whom we can learn from. The *Los Angeles Times* once reported on a factory worker from Detroit who worked overtime and scrimped so that he could donate hundreds of thousands of dollars to various colleges and universities. Often, we read about witnesses of accidents who risked their lives to help those who were hurt. While these people may not be Buddhists, their actions resonate with the Buddha's teachings. The common link among heroes is their ability to put the welfare of others ahead of their own. Their actions are not guided by personal gain or loss, but by peace of mind. These are all examples of putting the Dharma into practice, and each one of us has to find our own individual way of incorporating the Dharma into our everyday lives.

Follow through with our intentions

While it may be hard enough to be clear about what our goals should be, it is many times harder to have the stamina to complete what we set out to do. For instance, you may find that ideas in this book are inspiring and resonate with you. You might wholeheartedly agree that these pages contain excellent suggestions about how to live a life of affinity. But these ideas and teachings are meaningless if they are not put into practice. They are merely words on a page, unfruitful notions that exist only in the mind and not in life. Spiritual development cannot progress if we only think about doing good, but do not put the teachings into practice and experience them firsthand. Additionally, if the teachings are kept only on an intellectual level, there is no opportunity for their wonders to be manifested in our relationships—we will wind up helping no one. Having mental clarity and good intentions are important steps, but following through is what will truly make a difference in our lives and the lives of others.

Once, a monk who had achieved arhatship was traveling with his student. Carrying the bags on his shoulder and respectfully walking behind his teacher, the student suddenly thought of how he would one day like to teach the Dharma to all sentient beings. The monk read his student's thoughts and was embarrassed that he himself had never had such a grand desire to help all sentient beings. Thereupon, he asked the student to hand him the bags and he himself walked behind the student. The student just scratched his head and did what he was told. While walking in front of his teacher, the student had another thought, "Sentient beings are not easy to change, and the work of teaching the Dharma is arduous. I should just work on my own enlightenment." When the monk read the student's mind once again, he told his student, "Take my bags and walk behind me." The student had no idea what this was all about, but did what he was told anyway. From this story we see that while good intentions are to be applauded, they alone are not enough. We need to follow through with our intentions, otherwise our spiritual development and practice remains an idea, not a reality that serves to benefit both others and ourselves.

Sariputra, one of the ten noted disciples of the Buddha, gives us another example of carrying through one's intentions. In one of his previous lifetimes, he was dedicated to practicing the bodhisattva path and the precept of giving. He vowed that not only would he willingly give his property and possessions to others, but he would also not hesitate to give his body and life to those who were in need. The enormity of the vow shook the heavens and the earth, and a celestial being decided to test his conviction.

The celestial being transformed himself into a young man and placed himself on the path that Sariputra would pass along. When he saw Sariputra coming in the distance, he began crying loudly. Sariputra went up to comfort the young man and asked, "Young man, why are you crying?"

"Don't ask; there is nothing you can do to help. My mother came down with a deadly illness, and to cure her of her disease I need the eye of a monk. There is no way I can find a living eyeball, let alone that of a monk. I am afraid my mother will die."

Sariputra thought to himself, "I have two eyes. Even if I give him one, I would still be able to see." So, he said to the young man, "Don't despair. I am a monk and I am most willing to give you one of my eyes. I have vowed to practice the bodhisattva path and give alms. In a way, you are helping me to actualize my vow. Please take one of my eyes."

The young man refused to remove the eyeball himself and told Sariputra that if he was truly sincere about his offer, he should pull the eyeball out himself. Sariputra thought that was reasonable, so he gritted his teeth and pulled his left eyeball out. The young man took the eyeball and yelled, "Who told you to pull the left eyeball out? The medicine calls for an eyeball from the right eye!" At this time, Sariputra could only blame himself for not asking the right questions. Since he had vowed to practice giving alms, even if it meant giving his body, he decided to fulfill the young man's request. With determination, he took a deep breath, pulled out his right eyeball, and handed it to the young man. The young man took the right eyeball, gave it a sniff, and tossed it to the ground. He cursed, "What kind of monk are you? The eyeball smells so putrid; how can I use it for my mother's medicine!" The young man even put his foot on the eyeball and crushed it.

Sariputra might have been blind, but he could clearly hear what was happening. He let out a sigh and thought to himself, "The delusions of sentient beings are indeed hard to remove, and the bodhisattva path is not easy to travel. Maybe I should first work on my own enlightenment." At that moment, many celestial beings appeared in the sky and said to Sariputra, "Monk, please do not despair. The young man you talked to just now was here to test your resolve. You should not give up your practice of the bodhisattva path and alms-giving so readily." When Sariputra heard this, he was embarrassed that he had doubted and once again affirmed his resolve. Eventually, after sixty kalpas, he became one of the ten noted disciples of the Buddha and attained enlightenment.

The path to Buddhahood is a long one. During the journey, we are bound to face obstacles, and it behooves us not to give up easily. If we do, it is just like sowing seeds without bothering to give them water and fertilizer. Without nurture and the test of time, the chance of a plant blooming and bearing fruit is minimal at best. Thus, if we are to complete the goal we set out to achieve, we should be willing to do the "impossible" task and walk the "impossible" walk. We have to keep in mind that understanding and practice are equally important. If we continually put the Buddha's teachings into practice, one day we will discover that the Dharma and we are one. We will be living affinity and our lives will be truly joyful.

I hope I have succeeded in making the Dharma more relevant and accessible to you. Some people believe that to be profound, something has to be incomprehensible. This is not the case at all. The Dharma is something we all can understand and use. The Dharma is a guiding light that can help us to better evaluate the many and varied aspects of life.

There is a prevailing misconception that Buddhism has very little to do with living. Some people look at Buddhism as something that is mystical, unfathomable, and cryptic. This cannot be further from the truth. Buddhism is about life and is inseparable from life. My hope is that you all can blend Buddhism into living and mix the art of living into Buddhism.

❧ Notes ❧

1. Literally, the word Sarvadatta means "giving all."
2. A bodhisattva known for recognizing every being as a Buddha-to-be; he greets them with the respect and reverence they should be accorded.
3. A famous general of the Yan State during the Epoch of Warring States (403–221 B.C.E.).
4. Located in Honan Province, China.
5. Located in central Jiangsu Province, China.
6. In those days in China, corporal punishment was an acceptable teaching tool.
7. Located in central Shandong Province, China.
8. (1886–1946 C.E.) A famous literary figure of Chinese society at the time.
9. In the old days in China, most beggars carried a stick for protection and to ward off dogs.
10. The Chinese art of arranging surroundings (i.e., furniture, architecture) in order to create a harmonious relationship with the natural and omnipresent flow of life energy.
11. A chiliocosm is an immense cosmos of incalculable expanse.

12. The word "notion" here refers to the mental construct of outward appearances.
13. "Recognized," rather than "transformed," is used here because nothing is really changed.

❦ GLOSSARY ❦

Agamas: Also known as the *Nikayas* in the Pali Canon; they include the *Long Discourses*, the *Middle Length Discourses*, the *Connected Discourses*, and the *Gradual Discourses of the Buddha*.

Amitabha Buddha: The Buddha of Infinite Light or Infinite Life. Amitabha is one of the most popular Buddhas in Mahayana Buddhism. He presides over the Western Pure Land.

Amitabha Sutra: One of the three sutras that form the doctrinal basis for the Pure Land School of Mahayana Buddhism.

Analects: (Chinese *Lun Yu*.) Confucius's thoughts.

Ananda: One of the ten great disciples of the Buddha. He is noted as the foremost in hearing and learning.

Anhui: One province of China; also known as "Wan." Jiuhua Shan (Mount Jiuhua) is located in this province.

Aniruddha: One of the ten disciples of the Buddha. He is known as the foremost disciple with a divine eye.

Arhat: Literally, "being worthy of." One who has completely eliminated all afflictions and passions forever.

Avalokitesvara: Literally, "He who hears the sounds of the worlds." In Mahayana Buddhism, Avalokitesvara is known as the Bodhisattva of Compassion. He is able to manifest himself in any form necessary in order to help any being. In China, he is well known as "Guanyin."

Avalokitesvara Bodhisattva Sutra: See Chapter of Universal Gateway.

Bai Juyi: A famous poet (772–846) in the Tang Dynasty.

Bhiksu: A male member of the Buddhist sangha who has renounced the household life and received full ordination.

Bhiksuni: A female member of the Buddhist sangha who has renounced the household life and received full ordination.

Bodhi: A Sanskrit term meaning "enlightenment."

Bodhicitta: The mind of bodhi or a mind seeking enlightenment.

Bodhisattva: "A being who enlightens." It refers to anyone who seeks Buddhahood and vows to liberate all sentient beings.

Brahma Net Sutra: A sutra that describes the stages of cultivation in the bodhisattva path, the ten major and the forty-eight minor precepts that should be upheld.

Brahman (also "brahmin"): The highest of four castes in ancient India. Traditionally, brahmans were teachers and interpreters of religious knowledge. They were also the priests who acted as intermediaries between gods, the world, and humans. They were the only group allowed to perform religious rituals.

Buddha: Literally, "awakened one." When the term "the Buddha" is used, it usually refers to the historical Buddha (see Sakyamuni Buddha).

Buddha-nature: The inherent nature that exists in all beings. It refers to the ability to achieve Buddhahood.

Buddhahood: The attainment and expression that characterizes a Buddha. It is the goal of all beings.

Cause and condition: The primary cause (cause), which is like the seed of a plant, and the secondary cause (condition), which is like the elements of soil, water, sunlight, and so forth.

Cause and effect: See Law of cause and effect.

Chan: The Chinese transliteration of the Sanskrit term *dhyana*; it refers to meditative concentration.

Chan Master Baizhang: Also known as Baizhang Huaihai. He studied with Chan Master Mazu Daoyi and established the system in which the sangha provides its own daily necessities by cultivating vegetables.

Chan Master Muzhou Daoming: See Chen Zunsu.

Chan School: School of Chinese Buddhism founded by Bodhidharma. It emphasizes the activation of intrinsic wisdom and teaches that enlightenment consists of clarifying the mind and seeing one's own true nature. Another major statement of Chan School is that Dharma is wordlessly transmitted from mind to mind.

Chapter of Universal Gateway: Refers to the twenty-fifth chapter of the *Lotus Sutra*. Also known as the *Avalokitesvara Bodhisattva Sutra*.

Chen Zunsu: Also known as Chan Master Muzhou Daoming (780–877) after his renunciation. He belongs to the lineage of Chan Master Huangbo Xiyun.

Cheng Fo Zhi Dao: See *The Way to Buddhahood*.

Connected Discourses of the Buddha: (Sanskrit: *Samyuktagama Sutra*; Chinese: *Zhong Ahan Jing*; Pali: *Samyutta*

Nikaya.) So named because the objects the Buddha teaches include bhiksus, bhiksunis, upaskas, upasikas, and heavenly beings. The teachings also include several subjects such as the Four Noble Truths, Noble Eightfold Path, and dependent origination.

Cihang: See Venerable Cihang.

Cizang: See Master Cizang.

Cycle of rebirth: Also known as "cycle of birth and death" and "transmigration" or *samsara* in Sanskrit. When sentient beings die, they are reborn in one of the six realms of existence. The cycle is continuous and endless due to the karmic result of one's deeds.

Dayu: Also known as "Xia Yu" (2205–2198 B.C.E.). The first emperor of the Xia Dyansty, known as the first dynasty in Chinese history.

Devadaha: One kingdom in the Buddha's time, the mother country of Prince Yosodhara, ruled by King Suprabuddha, the father of Yosodhara.

Dharma: With a capital "D": 1) the ultimate truth, and 2) the teachings of the Buddha. When the Dharma is applied or practiced in life, it is 3) righteousness or virtues. With a lowercase "d": 4) anything that can be thought of, experienced, or named; close to "phenomena."

Dharma method of non-duality: One of the Buddha's teachings; it espouses the doctrines of no extremes, no distinctions, and equality.

Dharmakaya: Also known as Dharma-body. Indicating the true nature of a Buddha, also referring to the absolute Dharma the Buddha has attained. It is also one of three bodies possessed by a Buddha.

Dhyana: See Chan.

Diamond Sutra: *Vajracchedika Prajna Paramita Sutra*. The Diamond Sutra sets forth the doctrine of emptiness and the perfection of wisdom. It is named such because the perfection of wisdom cuts delusion like a diamond.

Documentary of the Warring Period: Ch. "Zhanguo Ce." Compiled by Liu Xiang during the Chinese Han Dynasty, which recorded important events of each state in the Warring Period.

Earth Store or Earth Treasure Bodhisattva: See Ksitigarbha Bodhisattva.

Epoch of Warring States: (475–221 B.C.E.) During this era, China was divided into seven great kingdoms. This epoch ended when the First Emperor of the Qin Dynasty invaded and conquered the other kingdoms, which resulted in the unity of China.

Five aggregates: Indicate form, feeling, perception, mental formation, and consciousness.

Fo Guang Shan: Monastic order in Kaohsiung, Taiwan, established by Venerable Master Hsing Yun in 1964.

Gatha: Verse.

Hongyi: See Venerable Hongyi.

Huineng: (638–713) Very influential Chan Master and Sixth Patriarch of the Chinese Chan lineage.

Jataka Tales: One part of Buddhist Canon, which describes the Buddha's practices of great compassion in his previous lives in the style of story telling.

Jeta: See Prince Jeta.

Jetavana Monastery: Also known as "Jetavana Grove"; located in the south of the city Sravasti. It was donated by Sudatta to the Buddha for the purpose of discoursing on the Dharma and for the gathering of the Sangha.

Jianzhen: See Venerable Jianzhen.

Jiuhua Shan: Also known as "Mount Jiuhua"; one of four great mountains for Chinese Buddhists, located in Anhui Province in China. An important pilgrimage site for Chinese Buddhists who venerate the Ksitigarbha Bodhisattva.

Judgment King of Hell: See King Yama.

Kalpas: Measuring unit of time in ancient India; a kalpa is an immense and inconceivable length of time. Buddhism adapts it to refer to the period of time between the creation and recreation of the worlds.

Kapilavastu: Ancient kingdom in North India, ruled by King Suddhodana.

Karma: Means "work, action, or deeds" and is related to the law of cause and effect. All deeds, whether good or bad, produce effects. The effects may be experienced instantly or they may not come to fruition for many years or even many lifetimes.

Kausala: Kingdom of India in Buddha's time.

King Suddhodana: Father of Prince Siddhartha and the ruler of Kingdom Kapilavastu.

King Virudhaka: One ruler of Kausala in the Buddha's time. Son of King Prasenajit, he killed many members of the Sakya tribe after inheriting the throne.

King Yama: Also known as Judgment King of Hell.

Ksitigarbha Bodhisattva: Also known as the Earth Store or Earth Treasure Bodhisattva. One of the great Bodhisattvas of Mahayana Buddhism. Ksitigarbha Bodhisattva vowed to remain in hell until all sentient beings are released from it.

Ksullapanthaka: One of the Buddha's disciples. He had a dull intellect and could not memorize any of Buddha's discourses. Knowing this, the Buddha instructed him to cleanse the filth within his mind while doing various cleaning chores. Following that instruction, he later attained great cultivation and eventually Arhatship.

Law of cause and effect: Most basic doctrine in Buddhism, which explains the formation of all relations and connections in the world. This law means that the arising of each and every phenomenon is due to its own causes and conditions, and the actual form, or appearance, of all phenomena is the effect.

Longman gorge: Famous Buddhist site in China, located in the south of City Luoyang, Henan Province. At this site, there are 1352 caves and 97,000 Buddhist sculptures.

Lu Fangweng: Also known as "Lu You." A famous poet and official scholar in the Chinese Song Dynasty.

Lun Yu: Chinese version of Confucius's *Analects*.

Luoyang: Ancient capital of several dynasties in Chinese history. It is located on the north side of the Luo River.

Lu You: See Lu Fangweng.

Mahakasyapa: One of the ten great disciples of the Buddha, known as the foremost practitioner of asceticism and regarded as the chief of the Buddhist order.

Mahakatyayana: One of the ten great disciples of the Buddha, known as the best debater.

Mahayana: Literally, "Great Vehicle." One of the three main traditions of Buddhism (the other being Theravada and Tantra). Mahayana Buddhism stresses that helping other sentient beings to achieve enlightenment is as important as self-liberation.

Marpa: (1012–1097) Famous master in the lineage of Tibetan Buddhism. Disciple of Naropa, he was the teacher of Milarepa and founder of the Bkah-brgyud-pa School. He also studied the teaching of Mahamudra under Maitri's instruction.

Master Cizang: Korean monastic who came to China in 634 (during the Chinese Tang Dyansty) to study the Dharma and returned to Korea in 643.

Master Xuanzang: (602–664) Great master in the Chinese Tang Dynasty. One of four great translators in Buddhist history. Studied in India for seventeen years and was responsible for bringing many collections of works, images, and pictures, as well as one hundred and fifty relics to China from India.

Maudgalyayana: One of the ten great disciples of the Buddha. Known as the foremost in supernatural powers.

Meru: See Mount Sumeru.

Middle Way: Teaching of Sakyamuni Buddha, which teaches the avoidance of all extremes.

Milarepa: Or Milaraspa (1038?–1122). One of the great achievers in the lineage of Tibetan Buddhism, and the chief disciple of Marpa. His work is known as *Ten Thousand Songs of Milarepa*.

Ming Dynasty: (1368–1644) Compared with other Chinese dynasties, Buddhism was declining during the Ming, but still there were some great masters to inherit the Dharma transmission.

Mount Jiuhua: See Jiuhua Shan.

Mount Sumeru: Or Mt. Meru; according to Buddhist cosmology it is the center of our world.

Naropa: (1016–1100) One of the great Indian teachers, disciple of Tilopa (988–1069) and teacher of Marpa.

Nirvana: (Pali, *nibbana*.) In Buddhism, refers to absolute extinction of individual existence, or of all afflictions and desires; state of liberation, beyond birth and death. Final goal in Buddhism.

Noble Eightfold Path: Basic doctrines of Buddhism. Indicate right understanding (right view), right thought, right speech, right action, right livelihood, right effort, right mindfulness, and right meditative concentration.

North Qi Dynasty: One of the kingdoms in the period of Chinese Southern and Northern Dynasties. Total regency lasted for twenty-eight years, experienced five emperors, and went through three generations.

Peng Zu: According to Chinese legend, he had a life span of eight hundred years.

Prince Jeta: Prince of the kingdom of Sravasti, son of King Prasenajit. Killed by his brother, Virudhaka.

Princess Yasodhara: Wife of Prince Siddhartha; also became one of the female disciples of Sakyamuni Buddha.

Pure Land: Another term for a Buddha realm, which is established by the vows and cultivation of one who has achieved enlightenment.

Pure Land School: One school of Chinese Buddhism, which emphasizes the concept of the pure land and being reborn there through the Dharma method of reciting a Buddha's name.

Putuo Shan: Also known as "Mount Putuo." One of the four most famous mountains in China, located in Zhejiang Province. Considered the sacred mountain of Avalokitesvara Bodhisattva.

Qu Yuan: (343–290 B.C.E.) Famous Chinese official scholar and literate of the Chu State in the Epoch of Warring States. His great literary achievements had a deep impact on Chinese literature.

Saha world: Literally, "saha" means endurance. Indicates the present world where we reside, which is full of suffering to be endured. The beings in this world endure suffering and afflictions due to their greed, anger, hatred, and ignorance.

Sakyamuni Buddha: (581–501 B.C.E.) Historical founder of Buddhism. He was born the Prince of Kapilavastu, son of King Suddhodana and his mother, Maya, who died shortly after his birth. At the age of twenty-nine, after he had been moved by the suffering of the sick and the aged, he left the royal palace and his family to search for the meaning of existence. At the age of thirty-five, he attained enlightenment under the bodhi tree. He then spent the next forty-five years expounding his teachings, which include the Four Noble Truths, the Eightfold Noble Path, the Law of Cause and Effect, and Dependent Origination. At the age of eighty, he entered the state of parinirvana.

Samyuktagama Sutra: See *Connected Discourses of the Buddha*.

Samyutta Nikaya: See *Connected Discourses of the Buddha*.

Samsara: See cycle of rebirth.

Sangha: One of the Triple Gems. Indicates the Buddhist community, including both monastics and laypersons.

Sariputra: One of the Buddha's ten great disciples, well known as the foremost in wisdom.

Six perfections: Also known as the six paramitas, which include the perfections of giving (*dana*), upholding precepts (*sila*), patience (*ksanti*), diligence (*virya*), meditation (*dhyana*), and wisdom (*prajna*).

Sixth Patriarch of the Chan School: Indicates Chan Master Huineng (see Huineng).

Six realms of existence: Indicate the six places of existence; the realms of heaven, asura, human, animal, hungry ghost, and hell.

Song Dynasty: (960–1277/8) Divided into two periods: one called "the Northern Song," and the other "the Southern Song." During this dynasty, Buddhism experienced integration within itself, and also melded within itself the characteristics of Confucianism and Daoism.

Sravasti: Famous Buddhist site, today located in Mahet city, Nepal. In the Buddha's time, King Prasenajit ruled there, and the Buddha lived and gave discourses on the Dharma there for twenty-five years in total.

Sudatta: In the Buddha's time, he was an elder of the city of Sravasti and an administrator of King Prasenajit. He built the Jetavana Grove for the Buddha.

Suddhodana: See King Suddhodhana.

Sui Dynasty: Its regency lasted for only thirty-seven years, from 581–618, and experienced three emperors.

Sutra: The discourses of the Buddha; one of the Tripitaka (three baskets).

Tang Dynasty: (618–907) One of the most important and brilliant periods in Chinese cultural history, and considered one of the greatest eras of Chinese civilization in both religion and the arts. Also considered the golden age of Chinese Buddhism.

Tantric School: One of three major traditions in Buddhism. Among the three major traditions (Theravada, Mahayana, and Tantric), the Tantric School was the one developed last in Indian Buddhism.

Tao Yuanming: Famous Chinese poet (372–427) in Chinese Eastern Jin Dynasty; also known as "Tao

Qian." His famous work is known as the *Collection of Tao Yuanming*.

Ten directions: In Buddhism, this term is used to refer to everywhere, indicating the eight points of the compass (north, west, east, south, southeast, southwest, northeast, and northwest) plus the zenith and nadir.

The four great all-embracing virtues: Also known as "four Means of Embracing," which are four methods that bodhisattvas use to guide sentient beings to the path of liberation. They are: 1) giving; 2) kind words; 3) altruism and beneficence; 4) adapting the self to others (or sympathy and empathy).

The Way to Buddhahood: Ch. *Cheng Fo Zhi Dao*. The work of Venerable Yin-shun, translated by Dr. Wing H. Yeung and published by Wisdom Publications in 1998.

Three poisons: Indicate greed, anger, and ignorance, the are three major elements that cause all afflictions and sufferings.

Trayastrimasa Heaven: Also known as "the Thirty-third Heaven," located on the top of Mt. Sumeru according to Buddhist cosmology.

Ullambana: Traditional Buddhist ritual in which sutras are recited to soothe the torments of the deceased in the lower realms of existence, e.g., the realms of the hellish beings and the hungry ghost.

Venerable Cihang: Famous master in the twentieth century (1895–1954). Contributed greatly to the reformation of Chinese Buddhism in the early part of the century. He studied the Dharma under Master Taixu's instruction.

Venerable Hongyi: (1880–1942) Famous master of the Nanshan Vinaya School in Chinese Buddhism. Before joining monkhood, he was a famous artist and musician in contemporary China.

Venerable Jianzhen: (687–763) Famous master in the Tang Dynasty; also known as the founder of Vinaya School of Japanese Buddhism.

Venerable Yinguang: (1862–1940) Famous master of the Pure Land School in the twentieth century; also known as the Thirteenth Patriarch of the Pure Land School in Chinese Buddhism.

Vimalakirti: One of the Buddha's lay disciples, an elder of the city of Vaisali. Achieved a great attainment of cultivation.

Vimalakirti Sutra: The main purpose of this sutra is to clarify the methods of practice for liberation that Vimalakirti has achieved and to explain the practices of the Mahayana bodhisattva and the virtues the layperson should strive to attain.

Vinaya School: One school of Chinese Buddhism; it emphasizes the importance of upholding precepts and the One-vehicle teaching.

Virudhaka: See King Virudhaka.

Wang Yangming: Also known as "Wang Shoujen" (1472–1528); a famous Confucian scholar in the Ming Dynasty.

Warring States: See Epoch of Warring States.

Western Pure Land: Realm where Amitabha Buddha presides. Came into existence due to Amitahba Buddha's forty-eight great vows. Sentient beings can make a vow to be reborn there where they can practice without obstructions until they attain enlightenment.

World of Ultimate Bliss: Same as the Western Pure Land.

Xia Yu: See Dayu.

Xuanzang: See Master Xuanzang.

Yama: See King Yama.

Yan Hui: Also known as "Yanzu"; born in the Epoch of the Spring and Autumn. He was the most virtuous of the disciples of Confucius.

Yasodhara: See Princess Yasodhara.

Yellow River: Second longest river in China. It can be traced to a source high in the majestic Yagradagze Mountains in the nation's far west. It loops north, bends south, and flows east for 5,464 km until it empties into the sea, draining a basin of 745,000 sq. km, which nourishes 120 million people. Millennia ago, the Chinese civilization emerged from the central region of this basin.

Zhanguo Ce: See *Documentary of the Warring Period*.

Zhaozhou: A famous Chan master in the Tang Dynasty; also known as Zhaozhou Congren (778–897).

Zhong Ahan Jing: See *Connected Discourses of the Buddha*.

**From the Four Noble Truths
to the Four Universal Vows**

Handing Down the Light
The Biography of Venerable Master Hsing Yun

Humanistic Buddhism
A Blueprint for Life

Humble Table, Wise Fare
Hospitality for the Heart

Let Go, Move On
Between Ignorance and Enlightenment

A Life of Pluses and Minuses
Between Ignorance and Enlightenment

The Lion's Roar
*Actualizing Buddhism in Daily Life and
Building the Pure Land in Our Midst*

Lotus in the Stream
Essays in Basic Buddhism

A Moment, A Lifetime
Between Ignorance and Enlightenment

Of Benefit to Oneself and Others
A Critique of the Six Perfections

**On Buddhist Democracy, Freedom,
and Equality**

Only a Great Rain
A Guide to Chinese Buddhist Meditation

The Philosophy of Being Second

**Understanding the Buddha's
Light Philosophy**

Where Is Your Buddha Nature
Stories to Instruct and Inspire